The Women of Ukraine

Stories of Hope and Courage in a War-torn Country

Christopher Briscoe

For Lyuda

The Women of Ukraine

Author's Note

In the early weeks of Russia's invasion of Ukraine, I crossed the border from Poland, stepping into a country under siege. Many miles felt precarious, some of the routes sketchy, with checkpoints and faces etched with exhaustion. But the stories waiting to be told drew me deeper. I returned again in 2023 and 2024, witnessing a nation scarred yet steadfast. Through these journeys, I came to understand the unyielding spirit of the Ukrainian people—and most profoundly, the women who have carried the weight of war on their shoulders. This book is a testament to their courage and resilience, as seen through the lens of my travels and their extraordinary lives. ~ CB

The Stories I Carry

When the first missiles struck Ukraine in February 2022, a nation braced itself for a storm of unimaginable brutality. Amid the chaos, it wasn't only soldiers who stood up to fight; it was the women. Their stories, often overlooked, hold the weight of a nation's endurance. Women have become the backbone of Ukraine's resistance, their strength woven into the fabric of survival, hope, and resilience.

This book is about them—the women of Ukraine. It is a tapestry of lives lived in wartime, where ordinary women are thrust into extraordinary roles. They are soldiers defending the skies, bakers feeding communities under siege, surgeons stitching together shattered bodies, and weavers crafting camouflage nets for frontline soldiers. These women don't see themselves as heroic, yet their actions echo far beyond the war-torn cities and villages. They redefine courage and rewrite the narrative of war.

Take Natalia, for example. Dubbed "The Iron Lady," she operates anti-aircraft systems, intercepting incoming Russian drones in the dead of night. Her precision and focus shield cities from destruction, her work a quiet but essential act of defiance. Or Hanna, a blind woman in Lviv, whose hands tirelessly weave camouflage nets. Her impairment, once a source of self-doubt, has become irrelevant in the face of purpose. "Here, I am useful," she told me.

There's Oleksandra Mostepan, a plastic surgeon who left a glamorous life in Monaco to return to Ukraine, trading luxury for a battlefield hospital. She co-founded Uplus, a company dedicated to creating advanced prosthetics for wounded soldiers. Every limb she helps craft is a testament to hope—not just for the individual but for a nation that refuses to accept permanent loss.

Women like Svitlana, a baker in Lviv, find their own ways to resist. She rises early, kneading dough even as air raid sirens wail in the background. The bread, simple yet vital, has become a symbol of continuity, proof that life carries on even amid destruction.

And then there's Kateryna, known by her military call sign "Ptashka," or "Bird." As a paramedic in the Azov Battalion, Kateryna endured the siege of Mariupol's Azovstal steel plant. Deep in its underground bunkers, she worked tirelessly to save lives with dwindling supplies, treating wounds with nothing but her hands and hope. Captured during the surrender of Azovstal, she endured months of torture, starvation, and confinement in Russian prisons. Yet even in captivity, she clung to her identity, hiding photo memories on a thumb drive in her shoe. When she was finally freed in a prisoner swap, Kateryna returned not to safety but to the front lines. "It's not scary to die," she told me. "It's scary to give up." Her story, like so many others, defies the limits of endurance.

These stories are deeply personal, yet they are universal in their themes. They speak of sacrifice and loss, of determination and creativity, of the quiet strength that comes from necessity. War is not new to Ukraine, but this war has cast women into roles that stretch far beyond the traditional. It has made them warriors, healers, and architects of the future.

But this book isn't just about heroism. It's about the cost of war. It's about Lyuda, who lost her husband to the conflict and now dedicates herself to supporting other widows. It's about the unspoken trauma that lingers in the shadows, the grief that doesn't dissipate when the last missile falls silent. It's about the scars that don't show, and the emotional burden of trying to hold a family together when everything around you is falling apart.

War, I've learned, is not always loud. Sometimes, it's the quiet struggles that leave the deepest impact. It's the mother deciding whether to send her child away to safety, knowing she may never see them again. It's the nurse who works a double shift despite exhaustion, stitching wounds while her own heart aches for her family. It's the grandmother who refuses to leave her village, planting seeds in the spring because she believes that there will be a harvest.

The Women of Ukraine is not an exhaustive account of every woman's experience in this war. That would be impossible. Instead, it is a collection of moments, of lives intersecting with history in ways small yet profound. These stories are as diverse as the women themselves, but they are bound by a common thread: the determination to persevere, to resist, and to rebuild.

As I wrote this book, I struggled with the question of how to frame their stories. Should I focus on their strength, their suffering, or the ways they defy expectation? In the end, I chose to let their own powerful voices guide me. They are raw, unpolished, and deeply human. They are not here to fit into neat narratives or inspire without complexity. They are here to be heard.

This book is my attempt to amplify those voices. It is a tribute to the women who have taught me what it means to endure. It is a reminder that even in the darkest times, there is light—and that light often comes from the most unexpected places.

To the women of Ukraine: This is your story.

~ CB

The Iron Lady: A Mother's Battle in the Skies of Ukraine

The cemetery is quiet, save for the soft crunch of leaves underfoot. The air is crisp, carrying whispers of the winter to come.

Natalia shifts on her feet. She wears fatigues, her blonde hair spilling from beneath a soldier's cap, the camouflage doing little to soften her sharp edges. She has come to

visit her brother's resting place, as she has often done since the Russians took Crimea. But this year, the loss cuts deeper. Last September, her son—her boy—in his twenties, was taken too.

Dmytro called her nearly every morning from the front lines, his voice a steady comfort at dawn. "Good morning, Mommy!" he would say. In one call, he was brimming with excitement about a girl he'd met online. "Mommy, I have good news! When I come home, I'll arrive wearing my body armor to propose to her!" But one morning in the summer of 2024, the calls stopped. He was 28.

Natalia is an Air Defense Anti-aircraft Operator. Most nights, she sits at her station in western Ukraine, ready and alert. She's been tracking Shaheds for months now, and with every launch, the stakes feel higher. Her team calls her "The Iron Lady," a title she has earned with her unflinching resolve.

It speaks not only to her toughness but to the weight of responsibility she carries each time drones or missiles are detected.

"When the invasion happened in 2022, it was all about tanks. That has changed. Now, it's about drones."

One night, the sky over Ukraine tenses with the ominous sound of approaching threats—20 Shahed drones, Iranian-made and supplied to the Russians, slicing through the darkness. These loitering munitions are notorious for evading radar, flying low and slow to exploit gaps in air defenses. They aren't fast, but they are deadly, carrying warheads designed for maximum destruction.

The alarm blares at 10 p.m., its wailing cry cutting through the night, announcing the arrival of the missiles and drones. Natalia doesn't flinch. She leans forward, her eyes narrowing as the screen before her lights up with red indicators—each one a Shahed, a flying bomb on a one-way mission. The drones originate from Russian-controlled territory, their erratic paths making them unpredictable. They can strike anywhere: civilian homes, infrastructure, power grids.

Natalia's fingers fly across the console as she adjusts the tracking system, her focus locked on the red dots creeping across the screen. The drones move deliberately, their slow pace unnerving. Every second counts. If she doesn't calculate their paths fast enough, entire neighborhoods could be obliterated.

She recalibrates the system, her hands steady but swift. Data streams in—altitude, speed, direction. Shaheds are trickier than traditional missiles; their unpredictable paths reveal their targets only at the last moment. Natalia knows this all too well. As her screen flickers with information, she fine-tunes the tracking coordinates, aligning them with Ukraine's defensive missiles stationed nearby.

Miles away, air defense systems roar to life, launching missiles skyward to intercept the drones. Natalia's eyes remain fixed on the monitor, inputting new data as the drones alter course. A civilian area now lies directly in the line of fire. She adjusts the calculations, her breath shallow but controlled.

"They won't get through," she murmurs, though she knows better. Some will slip past, no matter how precise her calculations. That's the cruel reality of this war—no defense system is flawless.

Flashes of light erupt in the sky as defense missiles find their targets. One by one, the red dots on Natalia's screen disappear—but not all. Two drones veer sharply, avoiding interception. Her pulse quickens, but her hands remain steady as she enters new coordinates. There is no room for error.

As the night wears on, Natalia's station is a hive of activity. Outside, the city braces for impact. Inside, The Iron Lady works, calm, focused, and fully aware that every decision she makes is a battle between life and death.

Dawn approaches, the sky outside begins to pale, but Natalia doesn't notice. Her focus remains on the screen until the last red dot disappears. The cemetery where her brother and son rest is miles away, yet it feels closer in moments like this.

Outside, as she waits for the morning trolley, the cool air carries the faint rattle of distant generators. Natalia exhales, her shoulders weighed down by exhaustion yet anchored by purpose. The trolley rattles to a stop, its doors creaking open. She adjusts her cap and steps inside. Commuters shuffle past, unaware of the battle she has just fought. For now, Ukraine is safe—at least for a few more hours.

Lviv, a city steeped in history, wears many faces, each telling its own story. In one image, storm clouds tinted pink by the fading sun loom over the city, casting an almost surreal glow on Svobody Avenue below. The towers of the town hall and nearby churches rise like well-armed sentries, their silhouettes etched against the approaching tempest. In contrast, the snow-blanketed scene of Lviv's Opera House exudes a quiet serenity. Horse-drawn carriages line the frosted streets, and bundled figures move among snow-dusted trees, their footsteps muffled by the fresh powder. These two moments capture Lviv's essence: a city that endures through beauty and hardship alike. Beneath the storm's intensity and winter's hush, the resilience of its people beats steadily, as timeless as the streets they tread.

Two photographs of a cemetery in Lviv, separated by time yet united in grief, tell a devastating story of a war that is relentlessly consuming the heart of Ukraine. In 2022, only months after the invasion, the graves held the beginnings of this incomprehensible loss, marked by a sparse scattering of mourners and flowers. By 2024, the same cemetery overflows with flags, flowers, and countless fresh graves—a grim testament to the war's insatiable hunger for life. Each flag waves not only as a symbol of defiance but as a reminder of the life buried beneath it. The earth, once a cradle of life, is now burdened with the toll of sacrifice, while the hearts of Ukrainians grow heavier with each passing day, emptied by the absence of those who fought and fell.

Top photo: Bogdana and Natalia share a deep friendship forged in grief. Bogdana lost her husband to the invasion just months after their wedding. Natalia lost her brother to the Russians. Then, they killed her husband. They comfort each other at the cemetery, surrounded by the flags of the fallen, bound by loss, but refusing to let sorrow break them.

Second photo: Ukrainian soldiers carry the coffin of a fallen defender in a solemn farewell. In this near-daily ritual, defenders and priests stand together, mourning yet another life sacrificed for Ukraine's freedom.

A mother wraps her arms around her children, holding them close as they say their final farewell to their papa. The grave is still open, the earth still fresh, but the weight of his absence has already settled on their shoulders.

Silhouettes of Survival

In front of a bombed-out building in Borodyanka, I met Larisa, a 64-year-old woman who has lived through unimaginable horrors. Her face, lined with grief, tells a story that words can barely capture. It seems like it's a part of the building—both beaten by time and war, yet still standing. Today would have been her husband Vitya's 65th birthday, but he was killed when a shell struck the courtyard where he stood. It began as a day like any other, with neighbors gathered outside, not expecting their peaceful town to become a battlefield.

Before the war, Larisa's life was simple and filled with happiness. She and Vitya shared a quiet contentment, enjoying every moment together. That tranquility was shattered when the Russians invaded. Larisa was at home when the explosions began, and in an instant, Vitya was gone, leaving her alone in a world that no longer made sense. On that same day, many lives were also lost in the courtyard, including that of a young man who died from his wounds the next morning.

After the shelling, Larisa sought refuge with nine others in a nearby building. She can't remember how long she stayed there—it's all a blur. When she eventually returned to what was left of her apartment, she found only destruction: shattered furniture, broken walls, flooding from damaged pipes and a life irreparably changed.

Larisa had worked as a nurse at a health center, but she retired after May, 2022. The stress and trauma have taken a toll on her health, particularly her vision. Now, she can only make out silhouettes, a cruel twist of fate for someone who once brought healing to others.

Yet despite all the loss and pain, Larisa's faith remains unshaken. When I asked how she could be helped, she replied with quiet resolve, "I hope God will give me the chance to see again." It was her only request. She believes that if she survived the Russian invasion, it was for a reason, a purpose that still awaits her in the future.

One Arm. One Broom. One Day at a Time.

Galina rises every morning at 4:30 a.m., long before the sun breaks the horizon over Horodok, a small village outside Lviv. She's 64 years old. An hour-long bus ride delivers her to the narrow streets and stone sidewalks of Lviv, where she sweeps every single day, seven days a week, with only a handful of days off.

By the time Galina boards the bus home at the end of her day, the city streets are jammed with traffic. When she steps back into her quiet village, most families are already seated for dinner.

Thirteen years ago, her life changed forever. A fast-moving soft tissue sarcoma forced a decision no one should ever have to make. Her husband had passed away the previous year, leaving her alone to face the diagnosis. "The doctors told me I had to choose—cut off my arm or die," she recalls. "I cried."

She was fitted with a prosthetic arm, but it was outdated and painful, rubbing her skin raw. Eventually, she decided it was easier to live without it.

Before her surgery, Galina worked at a bakery. She loved her job and tried to return, but baking with one arm proved impossible. Yet staying at home was never an option. "I want to work as long as I have strength," she says firmly. "Movement is life." Over time, she adapted, learning to live and work with one hand. She even taught herself to embroider—a skill she's proud of.

When she first applied for a sweeping job in her village, the employer doubted she could handle it. Undeterred, Galina traveled to Lviv, seeking a job with the city. The city manager was hesitant, too, but he agreed to give her a probation period. She had to prove she could keep up.

Day after day, Galina sweeps the streets assigned to her, earning extra by taking on additional routes. With fall's gusty winds and winter's ice, the work only grows more demanding. But she never slows down.

The Women of Ukraine

Her broom, made from stripped twigs, rests for a moment against against a graffiti covered wall. She stands, smiling despite her tired hand. The sound of distant cars rattling over cobblestones drifts by.

"My mother is 91," Galina says with a soft smile. "When I visit her, even though I'm 64, I still feel like a little girl when she hugs me."

Galina has three grown sons and four grandchildren. The youngest is just two years old. One of her sons, a psychologist, works with soldiers who've lost limbs in the war. Galina often visits his patients, offering encouragement. "Life goes on," she tells them. "If I can manage, you can too."

A cold breeze sweeps across the street, scattering newly fallen leaves over the path she just cleared. Winter is on its way. I ask her what the hardest part of her job is, expecting her to mention the rain or the struggle of cramming leaves into flimsy plastic bags. Her answer catches me off guard.

"Waiting for victory," she says without hesitation. "It comes at a very heavy price."

Galina wipes away a tear. Her words hang in the air, like the leaves that drift down from the trees—quiet, persistent, and stained with the echoes of war.

Creating Life in a Time of War: Olya's Story

My love for science began early. I remember being fascinated by biology in school — nature, life itself. University solidified that passion; I earned my bachelor's and master's degrees. My first job was in microbiology. It wasn't easy finding work fresh out of school, but I felt like my guardian angel was watching over me.

I spent a year working in a bacteriological lab, quickly adapting and growing. I learned the discipline of precision, of how even the smallest action can ripple out to affect something much larger. Eventually, I felt pulled to something new, a deeper way to connect my work with people's lives. That's when I discovered embryology, a field that would let me help people create life. I went through rigorous training, which was challenging during the first few months. Precision and thoroughness were key. I became an embryologist's assistant.

Embryology isn't what people might imagine. In vitro fertilization (IVF) doesn't happen in a test tube; it's a carefully orchestrated process involving meticulous preparation. Doctors prescribe hormonal therapy to stimulate the ovaries to produce several eggs instead of just one, as would occur in a natural cycle. This increases the chances of successful fertilization. Once the eggs have matured, the delicate process of egg retrieval begins. Guided by ultrasound, a thin needle is inserted through the vaginal wall, and the eggs are retrieved from the ovaries, usually under mild anesthesia. Once the eggs are safe in the lab, we prepare the sperm, making sure it is cleared of excess fluids, cells, and other particles. Only the healthiest, most active sperm are selected. This is a key step, as the quality of the selected material significantly impacts the likelihood of successful fertilization.

Finally, under a microscope, we bring them together in a Petri dish — the ICSI procedure, or intracytoplasmic sperm injection. This precise and complex process involves introducing a single, highest-quality sperm directly into an egg. The egg is carefully stabilized using a very fine micropipette, and then the sperm is injected using a micro-needle. It's a delicate moment. Any mistake could damage the egg.

If successful, the fertilized egg begins to divide, forming an embryo. Over the next few days, the embryo is observed in an incubator to ensure it's developing correctly. On the fifth day, the strongest embryo(s) are transferred to the woman's uterus. This final step completes the fertilization process and begins a new one — waiting for implantation and, hopefully, pregnancy.

Though the process is complex and demands concentration and skill at every step, it's always filled with hope and anticipation. Each stage has its unique significance, bringing the couple closer to their dream of having a child.

I remember the first time a woman became pregnant after I performed an embryo transfer. My hands were shaking. I could barely hold the phone when I called my mom. Telling her that I had helped someone become a mother brought both of us to tears. I knew she was proud of me. That was the moment I understood what my work meant. Each success, each new life I help create, is so much more than just a scientific achievement; it's a piece of someone's dream becoming real — a chance for a new life.

But war has complicated everything. Male defenders come to us to preserve their chance at fatherhood. I remember the calm, determined look in their eyes, asking us to freeze their sperm. They know the risks they face. They want to become fathers and have a desire to leave something behind — to create a new life. Some sign special documents allowing their wives to use their sperm to have children if the worst happens.

Women soldiers do the same, freezing their eggs, knowing the future is uncertain. Some military couples go through the process together. Each of them leaves me with a sense of profound respect and admiration for their courage, foresight, and desire to live and love despite everything — all of it a reminder of why I do this.

In the Arms of Uncertainty

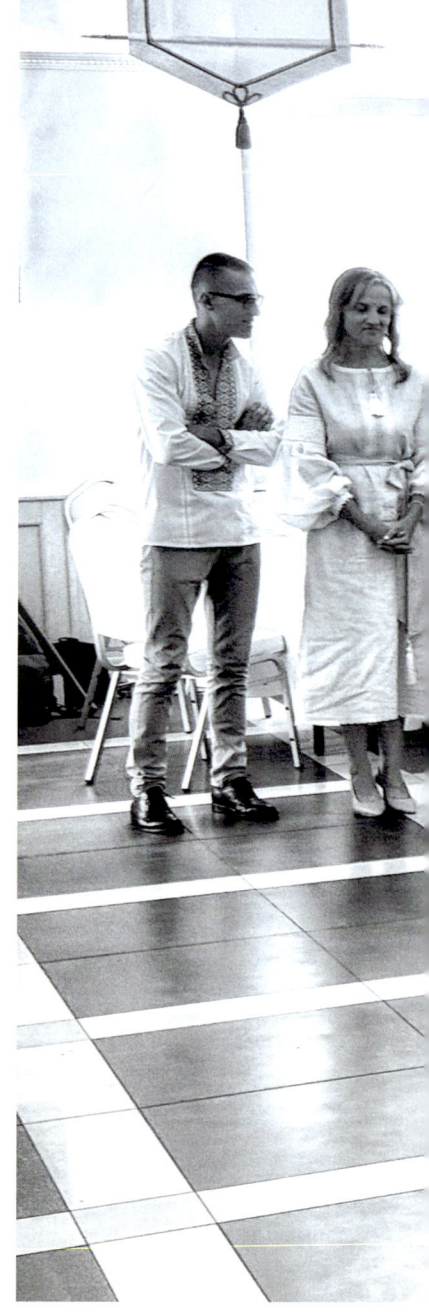

As Ukraine celebrates its 33rd year of independence, I'm invited to a wedding, an all-day event. The young bride, after a lifetime of preparation, wears a white-ribboned wedding dress so new it still has the price tags dangling from it. She hasn't had time to learn how to walk in her tall wedding shoes, so at the reception, she abandons them, preferring to go barefoot, skipping across the dance floor.

The reception is lavish, over-the-top for any Ukrainian budget. About 80 guests are seated at large, decorated round tables, piled high with traditional cold-cuts, salads, cheeses and bottles of wine. I realize that over 85% of the people in this room are women. The handful of men are either groomsmen on a two-day leave from the front lines or retired grandpas and uncles. Many of the women are widows. Without exception, every person at the wedding has lost at least one family member to the war. So many of the men in Ukraine

have either been killed or are on the front defending their country—and the rest of Europe.

A round-faced MC, with a booming voice, sounding like Bob Eubanks on *The Newlywed Game,* asks participants, "What's the groom's nickname on the bride's phone?" In another contest, he brings out a bathroom scale and weighs several guests at the beginning of the celebration and again near the end to see who has eaten the most. At this wedding, guests don't clink their glasses with utensils to encourage the bride and groom to kiss; instead, they approach the wedding table and drop to the shiny floor to give them a rapid succession of push-ups. A 68-year-old solid grandpa drops to give 'em not 20 but 30—the last 10 being one-armed push-ups. Later, a 6-year-old girl, with oversized glasses and red hair, drops and gives 'em 10.

I met Roxalana, an MD, several months ago as she delivered a cup of hot coffee to the love of her life's snow covered grave. Sitting on my right, she leans into me to explain that many of the wedding guests are linked through the cemetery in Lviv, having formed their own family through heartbreak and loss. "That older man who just did the push-ups, had two sons. The Russians killed one of them and cancer killed the other one."

Natalia, with light curled hair, who seems to be always smiling, reminding her friends, "I love you", sits next to Roxalana — another sister united in grief and survival. The first time I met Natalia, she was sitting on a small bench next to her brother's grave. Barely two weeks later she became frantic, trying to call her husband, a soldier on the front lines. After a cadaver exchange, she walked with his soldier-flanked casket into Lviv's Garrison Temple, and later to the ever expanding cemetery where diggers lowered him into a grave near her brother's.

I glance around the table. Lyuda is to my left. We became friends in 2022, some weeks after I photographed her husband's funeral, so gut-wrenching, I still tear up remembering it. Last week was his birthday. He would have been 50. Next to her sits 32-year-old Bogdana. When we became friends a year ago, she told me, "I may look like I'm okay on the outside, but on the inside, I am dead." Especially with her, time has helped heal. Tonight she's all smiles. I lean across to tell her that she looks like a movie star. Bogdana lets out a laugh and heads for the dance floor.

The groom briefly vanishes to change out of his suit and into his military uniform. It's not clear to me if this is because he wants to wear it proudly or if it's because he could get the call to return to duty at any moment — or both. The booze flows freely, but no one gets plastered. Responsible drinking seems to be the code, especially at the edge of a war zone. When the band cranks up the music, everyone is on the dance floor, joyous, celebrating the only thing worth fighting and dying for: love.

Lera, who has become the daughter I never had, sings into the hand-held mic, leading a long dancing line of happy women, snaking through the ballroom. I'm shocked with surprise, seeing her talent unfold, putting her recovering joy on full display.

As the night draws to a close, I find myself standing at the edge of the dance floor, watching the bride and groom swaying together, lost in the music and in each other's arms. There's a moment when their eyes meet, and despite the laughter and joy surrounding them, I see a flicker of something else—an unspoken understanding of the uncertain road ahead — the cold reality waiting outside these walls. But for now, they hold each other tight, as if clinging to these fragile moments of joy. In Ukraine, that's all anyone can do.

Amid the grandeur of an old Ukrainian hotel, a couple shares a quiet moment on the balcony. A kiss that might mark the beginning of their new chapter, but could also carry the weight of an uncertain future. In Ukraine, even love carries a shadow; he may soon have to trade this embrace for the front line.

The clink of a champagne glass echoes faintly from the room behind them, a toast to a fleeting moment of normalcy. Down below, an air raid siren wails, as if to remind them that life here never really pauses. They linger anyway. In this place, every moment feels more precious—sometimes because of the war, sometimes in spite of it.

The Women of Ukraine 26

Whispers from the Heart of Ukraine

Lyuda stands in the dimly lit church in Lviv, her eyes tracing the faces of fallen Ukrainian defenders—a somber mosaic of photographs. Men and women in uniform, their eyes are forever frozen in time. Each face holds a story, a family, a life cut short. Her fingers hover over the photos, brushing lightly over those who are strangers, until she finds the one she is looking for.

Her hand comes to rest on his face. Taras, her husband of 25 years. The father of her two children. She stands there, her lips moving in silent prayer, though no words can fill the gaping hole his absence leaves behind.

Lyuda doesn't move. Time seems to stand still, just as it did on the day she first heard the news. Yet here, in this sacred space, surrounded by the fallen, she is not alone. The weight of her

The Women of Ukraine 28

grief joins with that of so many others, each story woven into the fabric of Ukraine's struggle, each sacrifice a stitch in the heart of the nation.

Her fingers linger on Taras's image. His bravery, his love, his laughter—all of it feels so distant, yet painfully close. She whispers a quiet message, but it is not a final one. In her heart, he is always there, standing strong.

Taras is buried in Lviv's cemetery, in a new section called the Field of Mars, where an ever-growing number of Ukraine's defenders are laid to rest.

Lyuda visits her husband's grave several times a week, tending to the small plot with meticulous care. She makes sure the evergreens and bright yellow flowers are watered, and no weeds creep around the base of the cross that bears his name. His photograph, framed in waterproof acrylic, smiles back at her from beneath the Ukrainian flag that drapes the wooden cross. Mementos surround the grave—lanterns, candles, and personal tokens left by family and friends. She sits on the new bench nearby, quietly surveying the carefully arranged display, her fingers sometimes brushing the photograph.

As she sits there, Lyuda often speaks softly to him, her voice carrying stories of their children, updates from their life without him, and the emotions she can't share with anyone else.

She knows he hears every word. No one but Lyuda knows what her conversations with Taras are about. But they always end the same way: with her standing up, whispering goodbye, and promising to return.

The Church of St. Andrew rises behind a mural ablaze with flames, a tribute to Ukraine's defenders and the enduring strength of its people. Built between 1600 and 1630 as part of the Bernardine Monastery, the church once served as a defensive outpost beyond Lviv's city walls. For centuries, it has borne witness to life's most profound moments—weddings celebrated with joy and funerals

steeped in sorrow—its walls resonating with the rhythms of those it has sheltered. A fusion of Renaissance, Mannerism, and Baroque styles showcases its architectural evolution, while its interior, adorned with 18th-century frescoes by the monk Benedykt Mazurkevych, preserves the layered history of this sacred place.

Threads of Longing:
A Visually Impaired Woman's Journey Back to Ukraine

In Lviv's Rynok Square, women walk their small dogs as the morning light spills over a statue, covered in protective canvas marked, "We will admire the original after victory." A yellow tram clatters by, and nearby, another military funeral begins in a quiet church.

Up the worn steps of the library, Hanna, partially blind since birth, can only see silhouettes. The library room, framed by tall windows, is quiet except for the rustle of fabric. Hanna stands in front of a wall of fluttering white ribbons of cloth, weaving a camouflage net for the defenders.

"At the beginning of the war, we were in a panic. No one knew what to do. People fled from both the east and west because no one could tell where the enemy would strike next."

Hanna and her daughter fled, first to Europe and then to America. She stayed there for about a year and a half, but she deeply missed Ukraine.

"I am visually impaired, so I could not find work. I felt useless." Ukraine, with all its scars, was still her anchor. "I could not bear the longing," she says quietly. "I missed my homeland." Hanna returned to Ukraine.

Hanna's hands move quickly across the netting, focused on the task before her. "I was taught the skills to weave and now I know I am doing everything correctly," she says proudly. Hanna stands in front of the netting all day long, weaving in the bits of fabric to camouflage the defenders on the front. Winter is coming.

She pauses for a moment, brushing stray threads from her sweater. "Even in America, I was always cold," she says with a smile, half to herself. Outside, the yellow tram rattles past again. "But here, I am warm."

The Women of Ukraine 34

The Small Woman with a Huge Impact

In the bustling Lviv Volunteer Kitchen, you're likely to meet Julia. When she steps down from her stool, she stands barely four feet tall. But don't let her size fool you—Julia is a powerhouse. Her hands, in blue gloves, move with precision, swiftly slicing through meat and vegetables. Surrounded by the organized chaos of slicing tables full of pork, buckets brimming with tomatoes, and the constant rhythm of meal preparation for Ukrainian defenders on the front lines, Julia never misses a beat.

But her contributions go far beyond the kitchen. Julia is deeply involved in making the city more accessible for those with disabilities, a growing concern since the war began. With many soldiers returning home wounded and civilians injured by missile attacks, accessibility has taken on a new urgency in Ukraine. Julia's projects have helped reshape Lviv, ensuring the city is more navigable for all.

Her coworkers at the kitchen adore her for her tenacity and unwavering sense of purpose. They respect her not just for her work ethic, but for the heart she puts into everything she does. Around the large table that nearly fills the room, the atmosphere feels like family. Local grandmothers work alongside volunteers from America, the UK, Argentina— people from all over the world, united in a common cause.

Despite the somber purpose of their work, there's a warmth and camaraderie, with laughter and conversations filling the room as they chop, slice, and pack food.

It's no wonder Julia is respected by her colleagues. Her drive and dedication lift the entire team. The Lviv Volunteer Kitchen isn't just a place to prepare meals; it's a lifeline for those defending Ukraine, and Julia's contributions, both inside and outside the kitchen, are central to that mission. With every meal she helps prepare, she's not just feeding the soldiers. She's helping to sustain the fight for a future where no one is left behind.

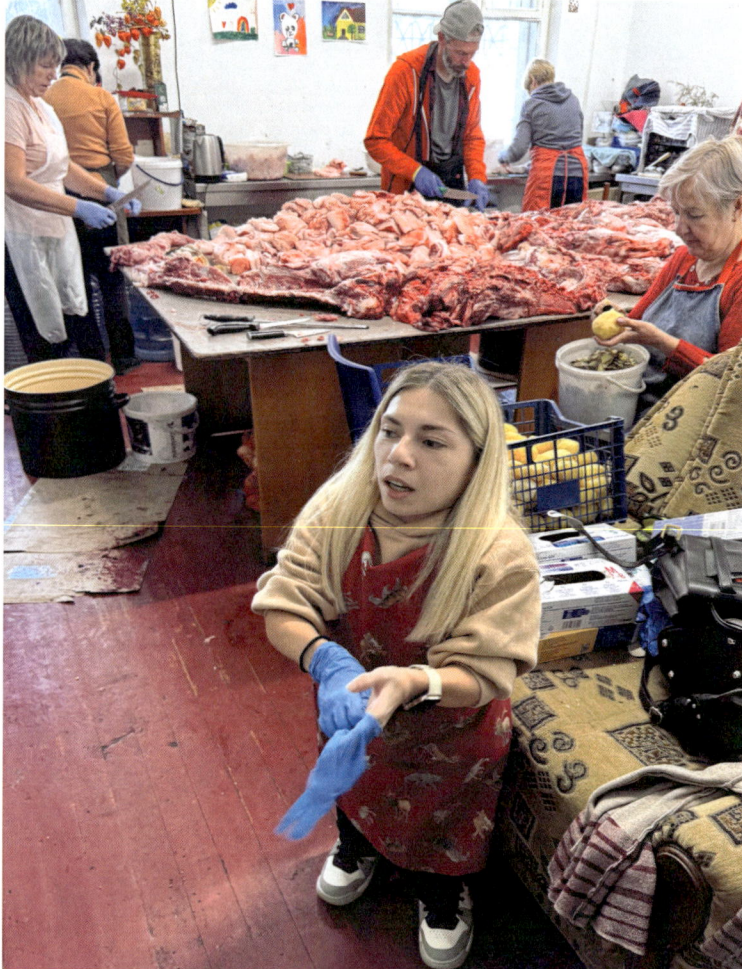

In the evening, the light dips behind the tower of the cathedral, casting long, dramatic dark shapes across the square. A woman's shadow stretches like a steadfast companion next to her, merging with the cracks of the cobblestone. The clock tower stands defiant against the sky. Pigeons scatter.

When the air raid sirens come, as they often do, the fragile peace feels like it could shatter. But Lviv doesn't stop. Neither do its women. They carry on, through air raid sirens and sleepless nights, through grief and exhaustion. They are silhouettes of resolve, etched into the city's shadows, moving steadily, step by deliberate step.

"The Soil Doesn't Turn as Easily as it Used To."

In the heart of Lviv, where centuries-old cathedrals rise against the sky and war shadows every street, life carries on. Along the sidewalks, amidst the chatter of travelers and the sound of passing cars, women gather, framed by buckets brimming with bouquets. Their weathered hands cradle blooms of defiance—reds, purples, yellows—vivid bursts of color that refuse to yield to the grey of uncertainty. These flowers are more than livelihood—they're offerings of hope, a living rebuke to a world so often dulled by grief. With the war dragging on, it's more than just a way to earn a little extra, it's survival. Many Ukrainians have lost their jobs, and even those with pensions find themselves at the market, trying to scrape together enough to make it through the week. Winter looms heavy without flowers to sell.

Oleksandra, 75, sits on her narrow corner of the pavement, arranging flowers she's grown in her garden. Her hands, calloused from years of labor, handle each bloom with care. She lives alone now, in a home she and her late husband built outside the city. "When I was younger, I worked as a cook and later in a hospital," she says, her voice steady. "Even then, I sold flowers." But even in hardship, gratitude softens her face. "Americans understand how hard it is for us now," she says. "And for that, I am always grateful."

Nearby, Iryna sits outside on a worn stool, bundled against the autumn chill in a thick jacket and a beret. Her hands rest in her lap, folded but not idle—hands that have tended a garden, turned stubborn soil, and weathered years of solitude. Beside her are small bunches of dried flowers, remnants from her modest plot of land where she grows parsley, dill, and carrots. "If my husband was still alive," she murmurs, glancing at the flowers, "I wouldn't have to sit here and sell these. The soil doesn't turn as easily as it used to." It's not a complaint, just a quiet truth. Her children, grown and with families of their own, mean everything to her. "I will manage somehow," she says, her voice carrying the pride of someone who has given everything and expects nothing in return. Today, Iryna managed to sell a few flowers. "I earned some money," she says, her smile faint but hopeful. "I will be able to get back my luck again." Her resilience hasn't been worn down by time or loss; it's been sharpened by it. Tomorrow, she'll return, just as she always does.

At the end of the day, when people pass by on their way to lay flowers at the graves of fallen soldiers, these women often give their flowers freely. It's their way of honoring the sacrifices made for Ukraine's freedom. Oleksandra, Iryna, and others like them don't just sell flowers—they embody the strength of a nation.

Even the rain cannot keep them away. Women stand their ground in flimsy plastic raincoats, selling whatever they can—flowers, fruits, vegetables—offering a piece of their lives to passersby. Their faces speak of quiet determination, a defiance that mirrors the blooms they sell.

Lace Curtains, Cracked Walls

The window, a relic of what was once a proud building, now stands as both a witness and a monument in the heart of Ukraine. Its cracked glass and peeling paint tell of years weathered under the strain of time, war, and the heavy weight of uncertainty. Through the smudged panes, the reflection of a weary city gazes back, resilient but scarred. Behind the lace curtain, fragile and yellowed with age, there remains a sense of dignity, as if it is shielding not just the room within, but the memories of those who once looked outside.

The wall, crumbling under the weight of history, reveals its layers—each flake of plaster a testament to the battles fought, not only in the streets but in the hearts of the people who lived here. Amid the decay, there's a different kind of beauty—the beauty of survival. Perhaps this window remembers the laughter that once echoed in these rooms, the whispers shared in secret, and the moments of fleeting hope that persisted despite the odds.

But there is something more. The face of a soldier, etched into the wall beneath the window, merges with the building's decay. His expression is both haunting and hopeful—a silent reminder of the sacrifices made, the defenders who have stood their ground. He is part of the structure now, woven into the fabric of this city, this war, this story. His gaze reflects the resilience not just of the window, but of Ukraine itself.

The weight of the soldier's presence deepens the window's silent witness. It is no longer just a relic; it is a testament to endurance. Like the city, it waits—through the passage of time, the march of soldiers, and the tears of those who have left and those who remain. In its stillness, it watches. It endures. It reminds us that these stories, etched in stone and glass, cannot be forgotten.

Etched into the Shadows of War

Lviv wakes slowly, the city draped in shadows that stretch like silent witnesses to another day's survival. On the edge of Market Square, the cobblestones shimmer faintly with last night's frost, now melting into the cracks. Lviv's rhythm feels unbroken on the surface—buses hiss as they come to a stop, heels click on the pavement, children's laughter echoes faintly from a nearby schoolyard. But every sound competes with the vibration of portable generators, a constant reminder that nothing is normal. The war has bled into the background of daily life like a watermark on old paper—faint but permanent.

A woman stands near the bottom of the stairs that descend into the underground corridor, a dim walkway carved beneath the busy street. By day, it hums with the footsteps of hurried passersby, a passage to somewhere else. By night, it often transforms into a makeshift shelter, where the cold concrete walls echo with quiet prayers and the faint rumble of missiles in the distance.

Her scarf is pulled tight, though the morning chill has long stopped bothering her. Her place on the steps looks as unyielding as the weight of history, a constant in a city swirling with motion. Every day she watches people climb—young men in heavy boots headed to volunteer for the front, babushkas carrying bags of bread or flowers for the cemetery. She has learned to recognize their moods by the pace of their climb: hurried, burdened, hopeful. Each step determined not to let the war weigh them down

Her small cup is a silhouette against the light, a fragile thing that reflects both scarcity and the quiet solidarity of strangers. Each coin dropped into it feels like a whisper: "We see you. You're not alone."

A woman hurries past the barbershop across the street, her steps purposeful, as though determined not to let the war weigh her down. The barber pole spins lazily, a strange contrast to the urgency in her stride and the city's air. Everyone is carrying something—hope, loss, or the will to keep moving.

Love, laughter, and a matching set of stripes. Even as the war rages on, some things remain beautifully simple.

I met a delightful couple in Odesa: Petro, 82, and Zhanna, 76, sporting matching outfits. They found each other a decade ago after losing their spouses. It was love at second sight... or maybe even the second lap. Zhanna loved taking brisk walks. Petro loved them too. One day, their paths quite literally crossed—and the rest is history.

Here's the kicker: they worked at the same job in their 20s! Apparently, they were too busy then to notice one another.

Now, overlooking the Black Sea, they stroll side by side, share laughter on park benches, and prove that love and style aren't bound by age or circumstance. War may rage on, but Petro and Zhanna are busy proving that love works in mysterious—and sometimes wonderfully delayed—ways.

Through Fogged Glass on an Evening Ride

It is evening in Lviv, and the night is quietly claiming the streets. Rain streaks the outside of the bus. The mingled breaths of worker-passengers within form a heavy mist of exhaustion that clings to the inside of the glass, refusing to let go, creating a veil that blurs the world beyond.

A dim golden light inside flickers gently as the bus navigates potholes, and the passengers sway along with its rhythm. An elderly woman sits slouched in her seat, her gaze lost somewhere as her hands rest on a frayed handbag, clutching it unconsciously. The long day has left her with no more thoughts to think—only a dull hum of being, waiting for her stop so she can climb the stairs to the predictable quiet of her flat.

Beside her sits another woman, bent slightly forward, her shoulders heavy with the burdens of the day. Her fur hat flattened, her eyes are about to close, to dream perhaps of simpler days.

Their figures blur together in the fog of the window. Their shadows are barely distinct from one another, connected by the unseen thread of shared weariness and concealed stories. Silence is their shared language, one that keeps them bound together in this metal shell that moves them forward through Lviv's dripping streets.

But outside, beyond the blur of the window, the city listens for the tremor of the war that never fully leaves. The bus's rumble over potholes echoes faintly of distant artillery, a reminder that even in the peace of a quiet evening, the war is still present, like a low pulse under the surface of normalcy.

In the faces of these tired passengers, there are stories untold—of sons and daughters fighting at the front, of bomb shelters crowded during the worst of the nights, of moments stolen between the routines of work and survival. The exhaustion in their eyes carries more than the weight of the day; it holds the weight of a nation at war, enduring, persisting, one day at a time.

The fogged window and the blur of exhaustion trail into the night, each soul leaving their tired imprint on the glass—a testament to the journey, an echo of the thousands of similar evenings that have come before and will surely come again, as the war looms just far enough away not to shatter this moment of sacred peace.

The Women of Ukraine 52

The Drone Makers
Fighting Russia from the Kitchen Table

As summer fades into fall in Ukraine, the devastating toll of the two-and-a-half-year conflict becomes ever more visible. Close to one million Ukrainians and Russians combined have been killed or wounded—a staggering figure for two nations that were already grappling with declining populations before the war began.

The number of Russian troops actively deployed in the invasion of Ukraine fluctuates, often estimated to be around 700,000. But that's just a fraction of Russia's total military strength—its active military force stands at about two million, with vast reserves and conscripts waiting in the wings. In contrast, Ukraine's active military personnel, while fiercely committed, are estimated to be about half of what the aggressor has and are gradually dwindling, as if Ukraine is bleeding out. It doesn't have enough soldiers to continue fighting a war that sees no end. The Ukrainian defenders on the frontlines are not young recruits either; the average age of male combatants is between 43 and 45, a stark reminder of the weight of this war on a generation that might otherwise be home, rebuilding their country.

Volodymyr looks over his white coffee mug. He's 28, but his eyes are serious. "I want to kill as many Russians as possible. One of my drones can take out at least three at a time." He pulls out his phone, scrolling through a series of videos, like he's about to show me clips from a recent vacation. In one, I squint at the pixelated black-and-white video, watching a squad of soldiers running for cover into a building. A second later, it explodes, leaving nothing but rubble and dust swirling in the air. It reminds me of a video game, but with real world consequences.

These drones are light and fast. Some can cover 150 kilometers in an hour, each loaded with a small, often improvised explosive. Flying them isn't easy—it takes hours of practice with online flight simulators to master the controls. But piloting is just one piece of the puzzle. Both Russian and Ukrainian forces are locked in a continuous high-stakes strategic battle of hunter and prey, jamming signals and tracking enemy transmissions in a fight for control of the air above the battlefield.

By day, Volodymyr works as an IT specialist at an army plant, a role that has earned him a military deferment. It's a job that keeps him close to the frontlines without being on them. His nights are spent in a different kind of battle; building the tools that will carry the fight to the skies.

Nearly every evening, Volodymyr and his girlfriend, Ira, hunch over their makeshift workbench in a small room off the kitchen, assembling drones in a space jammed with boxes of motors, wires, and circuit boards. A 3D printer clicks and whirs in the corner. The space serves as a makeshift workshop, one of about 700 small teams scattered across Ukraine, all working to build drones for the war effort. Each drone costs around $250 to produce, not including the handheld controller and FPV (first-person view) goggles needed to fly them. Some components are 3D-printed, but most are imported, mainly from China.

"China sells to both Russia and Ukraine. They don't care as long as they're making money," Volodymyr says, his frustration palpable. He knows the delicate balance this creates; China frequently threatens to cut off supplies, leaving him constantly scouring the internet and trade networks for alternative parts. It's a constant race against time, where a single supply chain disruption could halt their entire operation.

Despite the challenges, Volodymyr and Ira press on, working side by side. Ira beams with pride when she talks about Volodymyr's meticulous craftsmanship. "He's great at soldering. I'm not. I handle the larger parts." We watch him carefully connect the delicate wires that make each drone operational.

Every drone they build is a small victory. It's hard to imagine that this simple, cluttered room—filled with the quiet sound of a 3D printer and the smell of melting solder—could be such a pivotal piece of Ukraine's resistance.

Ira has family in Chicago and has visited the U.S. "I've been there seven times. I saw some of the Midwest, but I have no interest in living there," she says with a wave of her hand. "I know about the Kardashians. I want to live in my own country." Volodymyr had tried to visit the U.S. with her in 2018 but was denied a visa. The rejection still stings, but it hasn't left him yearning for another attempt. "I have no desire

to go to America", he shrugs. For both of them, Ukraine is home, and that's where they want to fight for the future of a country they refuse to abandon.

Born and raised in Lviv, Volodymyr has always been drawn to technology. Working in IT has been his career since day one, and even though his military deferment keeps him away from the front lines, he believes his skills are better used elsewhere. "I could join the Army," he says, pausing as if weighing the thought, "but I can kill more Russians with the drones I make. They have three times as many fighters as we do. That means I have to kill 3 of them for each Ukrainian defender they kill." There's no bravado in his voice—just a cold, calculated understanding of the role he plays in this war. Each drone he builds represents another chance to defend his homeland, and in that, he finds his purpose.

Our conversation drifts over cups of strong coffee and Ira's delicious homemade cherry pie. In Ukraine, especially in the cities, most people hold a university degree. They're well-read, and they keep up with the news—particularly American politics—because they know that much of their fate hinges on critical decisions made in the back rooms of Washington, D.C. Volodymyr is no exception. He's sharp, opinionated, and tuned into the political currents shaping his country's future.

He's doesn't mince words when it comes to his views about American politics. "I don't like Trump," he says plainly, though he quickly adds, "but the Left is weak." There's a pause before he continues, his brow furrowing in thought. "Will the presidential debates really change anyone's mind?" he asks, almost as if answering his own question. Perhaps it's a reflection of the cynicism that's grown in him, shaped by years of watching foreign powers toy with Ukraine's destiny from afar.

Volodymyr doesn't hesitate when it comes to his feelings about Russia. He's convinced that all Russians are inherently bad—a sweeping judgment that leaves no room for nuance. I suggest that maybe it's more about the character of the Russian state and its oppressive government, but he doesn't flinch. His expression hardens, and it's clear he's not willing to budge.

For him, this isn't just a war; it's the latest chapter in the long, bloody saga of Russia. He launches into Ukraine's violent history with Russia, from the famines and forced relocations under Stalin to the more recent invasions. "It happens about every century," he says, listing off atrocities as if they're etched into his memory. The scars of the past run deep, and for Volodymyr, they define his present. There's no separating the people from the regime—not when those people, in his eyes, have been complicit in so much suffering.

When I ask about the Russian Orthodox Church and its influence in Ukraine, Volodymyr's response is immediate and blunt. The Russian government doesn't really believe in God," he says with a sharp edge to his voice. "They just use the church to manipulate religious followers and to spy on Ukraine."

For him, it's not about faith—it's about power. He leans forward, his tone turning conspiratorial. "If you want to control people, you control their church." The thought hangs in the air between us, heavy with the weight of his conviction. To Volodymyr, the church is just another arm of the Russian state, another tool to impose their will on a population already suffocating under decades of propaganda and fear. It's a strategy as old as time, he says, a way to keep the masses obedient while masking their true intentions behind the veil of faith.

For Volodymyr, the Russian Orthodox Church represents a twisted version of religion—one that serves the state rather than the soul. It's yet

another battleground in this war, one that stretches far beyond the physical fighting into the hearts and minds of those caught in the middle.

As our conversation winds down, a full moon rises above the city. But, Volodymyr's focus never strays far from the war, from the drones he builds and the lives they might save…or take. For him, there's no room for doubt, no room for forgiveness, not with everything he's seen. His path is clear, shaped by the weight of history and the urgency of survival. In his mind, this war isn't just about territory or politics; it's about the very existence of his people. "Every drone we build, every Russian we stop, is one step closer to living freely in our own country," he says, his voice steady with the spirit that sustains Ukraine in this dark moment.

For Volodymyr and Ira it's simple: Ukraine is home. They will defend it, one drone at a time.

Oksana's Flights for Freedom

The drone lab smelled of burnt solder, a scent that lingered like a ghost after the team had left. Oksana and a crew of other techies met almost every night in the donated space, heads bent over tables cluttered with new and salvaged parts, lit by lamps as they pieced together drones to help arm defenders on the front lines. It was a place of trust, yet in Ukraine, trust was not always a given.

A new volunteer had joined them recently. Quiet, nondescript—the sort of guy who might disappear in a crowd. Something about him had felt off, a suspicion gnawing at the edges of their awareness, but no one said anything. In times like these, paranoia was easy to explain away. They needed all the help they could get and ignored the unease.

That night, the man left without his backpack. The crew didn't notice it—just another bag in a cluttered room. It wasn't until they were all safely home that they got the call: an explosion had torn apart their makeshift workshop, scattering the pieces like shrapnel.

By some small miracle, Oksana and her friends were safe. But the workshop—the heart of their quiet, determined resistance—was left a ruin.

Many of the drones Oksana and her team assemble can carry up to two kilograms of explosives. They're by no means large—only a couple of feet in diameter—but they're built to be sturdy enough to haul a payload and a battery capable of propelling them several kilometers to their targets. Most are one-way drones, commonly called "kamikazes." Some designs have a distinctive arch extending from the front, nicknamed a "mustache" or "stinger." When the stinger makes contact, it triggers a detonation.

Oksana's drones are meant to target Russian ground troops. She's clearly torn about this.

"This doesn't make me happy. Every drone I send out kills someone's child," she says quietly. "But the Russians are killing Ukrainians—my friends—the same way. When I watch the videos, I think, 'This could easily be Ukrainians on the screen. It could be my friends.'"

She pauses, then adds, "One of my best friends was killed by a drone. Ironically, he'd just sent one up. The Russians hijacked the frequency and sent it back, dropping the bomb on him."

Oksana pulls out her small phone and shows me a video taken just days ago. In the clip, a drone chases a few soldiers across an open field. Suddenly, there's a flash on the screen.

She pauses, collecting her thoughts before getting back to her point. "Many Russian soldiers have no idea why they're even fighting," Oksana says, frustration evident in her voice. "For what? Someone else's land?" She looks down at her phone, then back up, her eyes steady. "Until we win our freedom, I'll keep making drones."

Oksana knows her craft inside and out, and she eagerly describes the design of another drone—one that doesn't rely on the stinger. "This one detonates on any abrupt contact," she explains, her fingers tracing the shape of an invisible drone in the air.

"In the last year, drone warfare has changed everything," she says, a spark of intensity in her eyes. "We're always asking the soldiers what we can improve. Many of them say, 'We need two cameras: one for day vision, another for night vision.'"

Oksana explains the challenges posed by electronic warfare systems like the Russian "Repellent-1." This system can disrupt drones by jamming their control and navigation frequencies, affecting both enemy and friendly UAVs within its range. The ongoing challenge is to develop drones that can operate effectively despite such countermeasures.

"We work with another drone system that can handle bombs up to five kilograms," Oksana explains. "It requires a controller, a laptop, and a strong battery. Unlike the kamikazes, these drones aren't one-way; they travel up to twelve kilometers, deliver their payload, then return home."

She pauses, then adds, "But being tracked back is a risk, so Ukraine developed a failsafe. After delivering its payload, the drone's frequency shuts down, switching over to GPS. The GPS works with the onboard computer to guide it back safely."

Oksana elaborates on the Sokil-300 system, named after the falcon for its keen vision. This Ukrainian-developed system employs high-quality encrypted video feeds, enhancing operational security. It utilizes FPV (First-Person View) with laptops continuously shifting frequencies to counteract jamming efforts—a constant battle in electronic warfare.

Each drone is assigned a unique ID and firmware, allowing operators to distinguish between units. When a drone is captured, analyzing its frequency usage for the camera, controllers, and transmitters provides valuable intelligence. Regular firmware updates are crucial; neglecting them can lead to severe consequences. Fortunately, most communications are now encrypted, bolstering security against interception.

In the dim, cluttered workshop, Oksana and her friends are not just building drones; they are building Ukraine's future, piece by piece. Every soldered wire and every line of encrypted code speaks to their determination to protect what is theirs, to innovate where others might retreat. For them, these drones are more than machines; they're symbols of defiance, messages that carry both courage and hope across a sky filled with shadows. And as Oksana speaks, her voice steady and unwavering, one thing is clear: she will keep building, keep fighting, determined, until freedom is more than just a promise.

The Secret

The new building rises stark and unyielding in the cold night, its yellow facade dimly lit by bold windows. It could be anywhere—another orphanage, another place where quiet moments speak louder than words. But this one is in Ukraine, and inside it, a few dozen children live.

My friends and I pull into the driveway. Several inquisitive faces press against a window on the second floor. Some are smiling. Others are not. They've had their expectations dashed before. The orphanage director greets us warmly. Kids pile onto the porch to inspect our bags of goodies before carrying them inside.

Downstairs, several children sit at a long table, absorbed in art projects. Upstairs, a single hallway light flickers as we walk through the building. Rooms are lined with bunk beds, each one neatly made. Stuffed animals sit on pillows, their smiles frozen in place. Everything feels suspended, like a play paused mid-scene.

A little girl perches on the window seat. She is small, in pajamas covered with oversized polka dots. Next to her sits a massive bear, one arm across her lap as though trying to share the burden. Outside, the playground sits empty—two swings twisting in the wind, a slide dusted in thin dirt.
Her face turns toward the glass, her reflection folding into the yard's gray—as if searching for something that isn't there.

"Can you ask her what she's thinking about?" I whisper to Lera, my translator, not wanting to disturb whatever fragile moment I've stumbled into.

Lera kneels beside her. The little girl's eyes stay fixed on the barren yard. A few murmured words pass between them.

Finally, the girl turns her head just slightly. "Mom," she says in Ukrainian, soft as a secret that cracks open the silence.

Then she whispers something else, almost inaudible. "But don't tell anyone," she adds. "It's a secret."

She turns back to the window. Her small hands clutch the bear's paw, her head resting on its soft head, as if finding refuge in a silent protector. We don't ask any more questions. Some truths are sacred—especially those spoken by small voices, in places where warmth feels borrowed.

The Only Truth in the Room

I walk into the hospital room, the scent of antiseptic thick in the air. The corridor outside is lined with black wheelchairs, busy with distant conversations and the clatter of carts. Inside, the atmosphere shifts—quieter, heavier. Iryne, a soldier's wife, sits beside her husband, Artem, her hand resting gently on his. It's quiet except for the sound of weeping.

Artem, 40, lies in the hospital bed, his body crumpled into itself like someone carrying a weight too heavy to release. His face twists, every muscle clenched. His eyes squeeze shut, as if the world outside them is too much to bear. A brave defender of Ukraine, now raw and fragile, laid bare by war.

I hesitate, then reach out, placing my hand into his raised one. One of his fingers is missing. His hand feels like stone under my palm, as if war has scraped away not just parts of his body but parts of his soul. He flinches at the touch but doesn't pull away. Instead, his whole body shudders, as though that small gesture has cracked open something inside him.

Iryne strokes his head like a mother soothing a child. Her voice is tender yet insistent, laced with quiet desperation. "It will be okay, my love. They will take care of you. Don't cry. Everything will be okay. The doctors say you will walk again."

Her words are steady, almost rehearsed. Eight years of marriage, forged in the fires of war, have taught her how to comfort him. She knows exactly what to say, even if she doesn't entirely believe it herself.

Artem presses his lips tight, fighting the sob that forces its way out, a sound that feels more like surrender than grief. His trembling hand grips his shirt like it's the only thing tethering him to this world. The ghosts of comrades lost, the weight of survival etched into every line of his face.

I keep my hand in his, steady, though I have no idea what to say. His tears come silently, his face contorting with a kind of pain that can't be shed.

But Iryne doesn't falter. She holds him together with sheer will, her voice cutting through the silence. "Artem," she says softly, coaxing him back to the present. "What do you want to do after you're walking again?"

He hesitates, the weight of her question hanging heavy in the room. Finally, he murmurs, "To get up and walk."

"And after that?" she presses gently, her hand tightening around his. "What then, my love?"

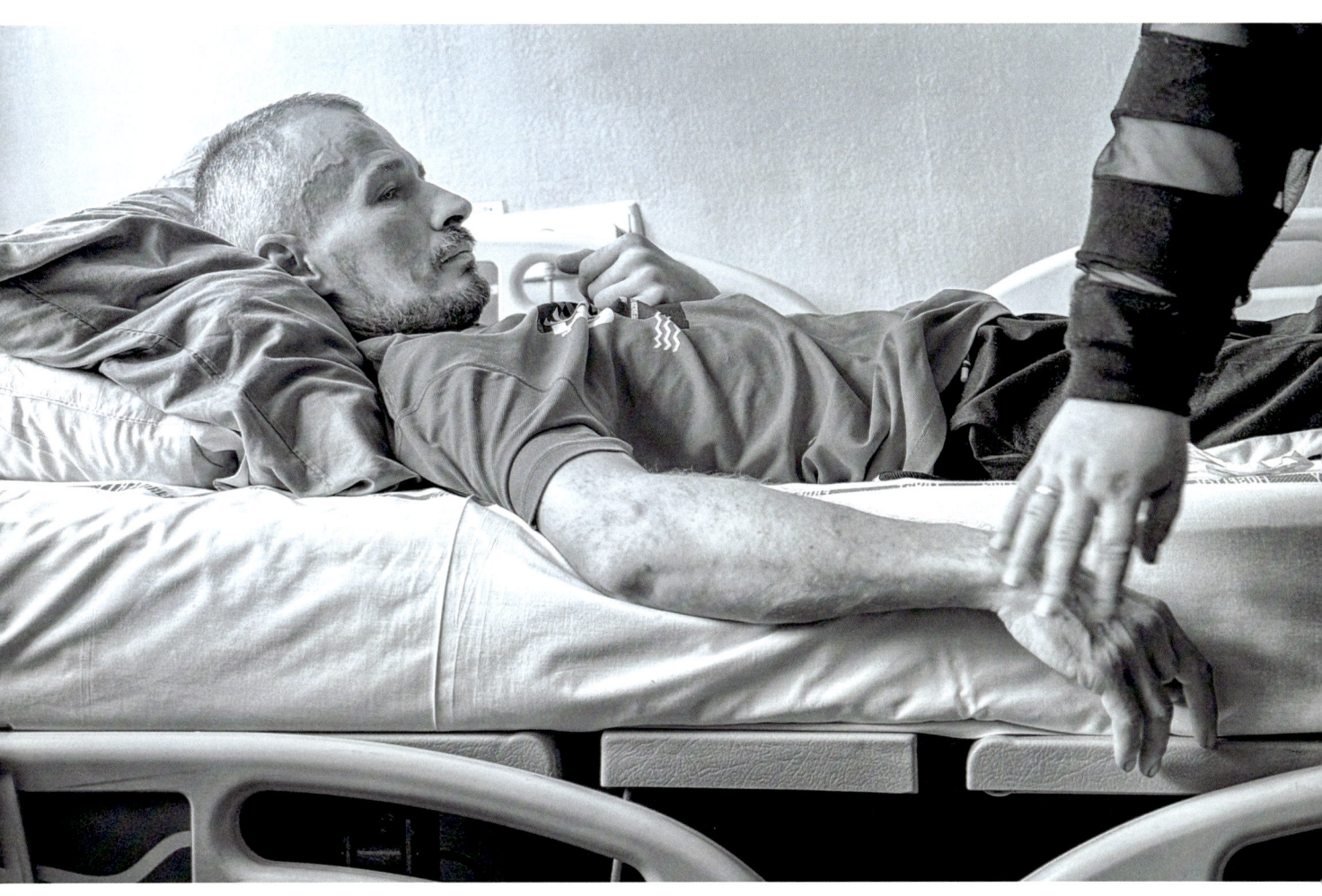

The words come slowly, almost reluctantly, as though saying them aloud might make them feel impossible. "Country," he finally whispers. His eyes flutter closed. The effort of speaking is exhausting and yet ignites something deeper within. "I want to take care of my country."

The room feels impossibly still, the air heavy with something unspoken. I slide five crisp one-hundred-dollar bills into his shaking hand, a small gesture from the GoFundMe donations entrusted to me. His fingers close around them slowly, trembling as if the simple act of accepting kindness is almost too much to bear.

Tears stream down his face—this time, not from pain but from gratitude. They come fast and without restraint. He weeps for the unexpected gift, for the reminder that people care, for the fragile thread of hope still connecting him to something beyond this hospital bed.

Iryne strokes his arm, whispering words of encouragement, her presence as steady as the bed beneath him. Together, they've faced so much; her strength is now the foundation he leans on.

We stay like that for a while; him wrestling with invisible demons, me holding on, and Iryne grounding him in the present with her unyielding love. In the silence, something shifts. Two strangers and a devoted wife, bound by a shared moment of vulnerability.

Outside, life continues with the sounds of footsteps, conversations, the clatter of carts. But here, in this small hospital room, his pain and her resilience are the only truths.

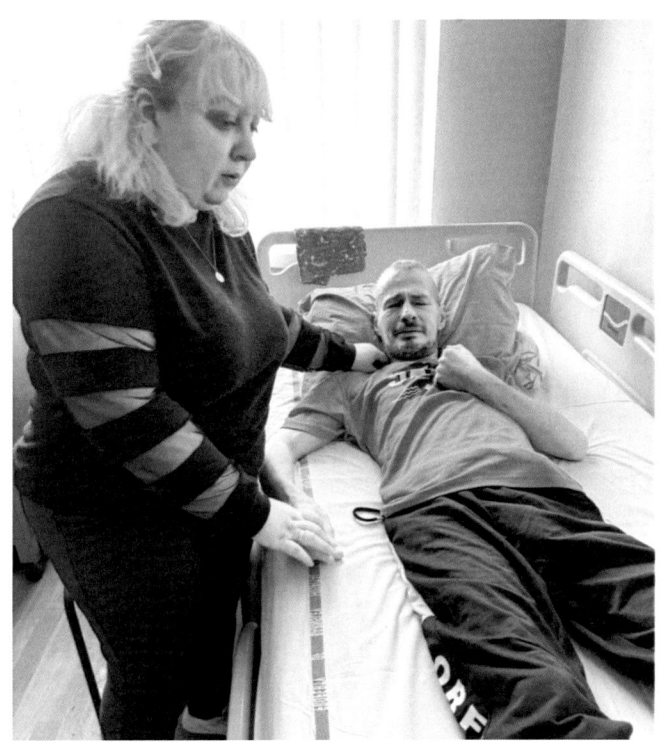

The Women of Ukraine 64

Bread and War: Baking Through the Pain

In battle-weary Ukraine, where grief clings to every town, Svitlana bakes bread, fulfilling a promise to the man she loved.

His name was Zhenya. He was 39. Svitlana, his love, was 41. They lived together in a small apartment in Lviv, where life followed a quiet rhythm. Every morning, Zhenya would walk through the city, searching for fresh bread to bring back to Svitlana for breakfast with their coffee. But no matter which bakery he tried, he'd always come home with a small frown and say, "There's no bread in Lviv as good as the bread you bake."

Then the Russians invaded Ukraine, and Zhenya went to war. One day, from the damp cold of a trench, his phone buzzed with a call from Svitlana. She asked if he was eating well. Over the line, she heard the crunch of an apple. He assured her he was fine, but then added, "The bread they give us here is terrible. It's often moldy. If I don't make it back, promise me you'll open a bakery so everyone will know how wonderful your bread is."

It was their last conversation. Not long after, Zhenya's unit came under heavy fire. In the battle, most of his comrades were killed. Zhenya hoisted his wounded commander onto his back, trying to get him to safety, but moments later, both were dead, their entire unit wiped out.

The news shattered Svitlana. The grief was overwhelming. But even as time passed, Zhenya's words about the bakery stayed with her. They echoed in her mind like a quiet whisper, nudging her forward. And then, the signs began to appear. One day, a butterfly, huge and out of season, landed on her hand. She watched as it gently drank from a teaspoon of sugar water. Not long after, a white dove flew through an open window in her cramped apartment, wandering calmly down the hallway, past her cat. Each time, she felt Zhenya's presence, as if he were urging her on, reminding her of their dream.

Money was tight. They had lived together for five years, and though he had proposed just days before being deployed, they hadn't officially married. In the eyes of the military, she wasn't his widow. There was no pension, no financial support—she was completely on her own.

But Svitlana wasn't one to give up. She worked tirelessly to make Zhenya's dream come true. She applied for a small business loan and, out of several applicants, it was her heartfelt essay that secured the funds. The bakery she opened is modest, tucked away on a quiet street where few pedestrians pass by. Still, she works with determination. In the mornings, the small kitchen is filled with the scent of dough rising, and flour dusts her hands, her apron, and the air around her.

Her hands, covered in flour, are her connection to Zhenya. Every loaf of bread that comes from Svitlana's oven carries a memory, a promise made in the trenches of war. The bakery is more than just a business; it is a labor of love, a promise she is fulfilling with every batch she bakes.

The Women of Ukraine

The Weight of Time

I sit on a sidewalk bench in Lviv, watching the old man shuffle along the cobbled street, clutching his worn red shopping bag. Each of his steps echoes the slow passage of time, like the crumbling building behind him with its bricks peeking through worn plaster like old scars.

The bag tugs at his hand, pulling him down. Above, a worn-out lamp flickers, barely hanging on. The city moves around him, indifferent, but he keeps going, his determination etched into every slow, deliberate step. He endures, even if no one else notices.

Except for me.

Beating the Drum of War and Will

The battered military jeep jolted forward. Ida steered it along a dirt road that seemed to stretch endlessly into the hazy, sepia-toned horizon—a lifeline and a trap in the same breath.

Ida was a Ukrainian drone pilot, skilled with both FPV drones and fixed wings. She had learned to maneuver them like extensions of herself, sending them soaring over enemy lines and through narrow corridors, guiding each machine with precision. It was a quiet skill that masked the intensity of her resolve. Now, in September 2024, she was steering a battered military jeep along a desolate dusty road deep in Russian-occupied territory. Her grip on the wheel was firm, but her eyes darted to the rearview mirror every few seconds, a habitual wariness etched into her since the first days of the invasion.

Beside her, a young recruit sat stiffly, hands clutching his rifle. He was barely out of the training center, two months in, green as they come. His nervous glances mirrored Ida's first months on the front. She'd been like him once, but now her gaze was calm, focused, her senses heightened by the raw silence that clung to the land around them.

As they rolled forward, the low rumble of the jeep was the only sound against the expanse of fields and abandoned homesteads—remnants of lives scattered by war. The dirt road stretched ahead, innocent and unmarked. There was no hint, no clue of the death lying dormant beneath its surface. When the front wheel struck the landmine, the explosion tore through the silence like a thunderclap. The jeep jolted violently, thrown upward and twisted as the blast ripped through metal and glass. Flames erupted in the grass around them, a fierce halo encircling the shattered vehicle.

The air was thick with smoke and scorched earth. Miraculously, the jeep hadn't yet caught fire, but Ida knew they had only seconds before the flames licking through the grass would close in. Every nerve in her body screamed at her to move, but she steadied herself, mind racing, already calculating their next step.

Ida fought the pain to keep her mind clear. She was trapped, a mess of broken metal pinning her down. Her left leg was mangled beyond recognition, but she couldn't think about that now. The new recruit managed to get out. She yelled at him, her voice raw, ordering him to get the Starlink transmitter from the pack and call for help.

He staggered, clutching his own leg with a compound fracture. Somehow, he got the transmitter up, his hands trembling as he keyed it. Blood soaked his pant leg, but he stayed on his feet.

Ida glanced at her own leg. She needed a tourniquet, and fast. Her hands were a mess, the left one burned and trembling so badly she couldn't hold the strap steady. She wrapped it wrong, inside-out, tightening it uselessly against her thigh. She clenched her jaw, forcing herself to stay focused.

"Get over here!" she shouted at the recruit. He stumbled over, barely holding it together, but managed to tighten the tourniquet around her leg. As he worked, she looked skyward, nerves tightening. Russian drones could be on them in minutes.

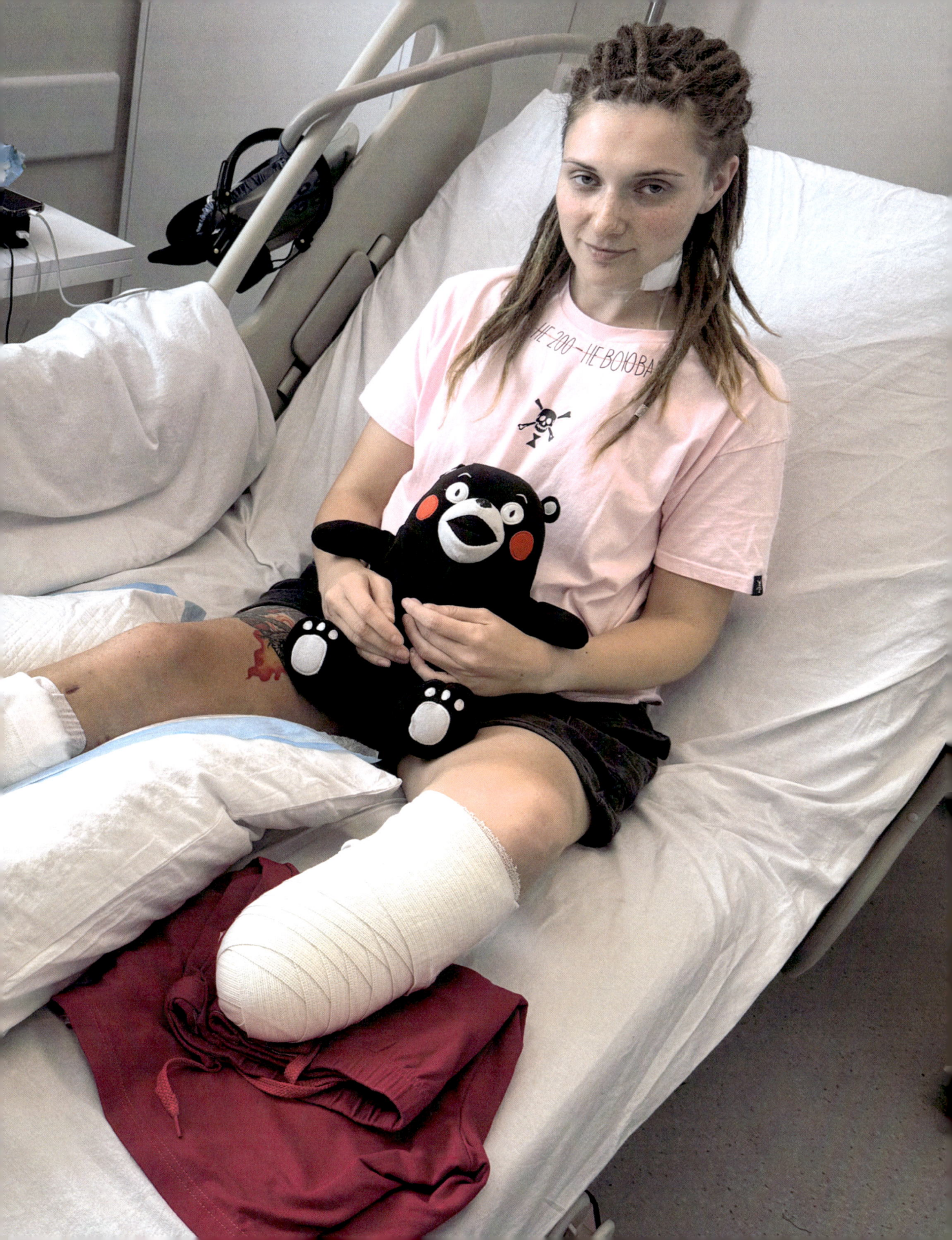

This road was inside enemy territory; they'd be a prize worth finishing off.

"Go to the back!" she ordered. "Grab the case of drone explosives. Get them clear of us." She watched as he crawled to the back of the wrecked jeep, pulling out the metal case, gritting his teeth as he dragged it away.

Ida looked down at her leg again, twisted and broken in ways she couldn't recognize. She was losing blood. Every minute was slipping away, yet all she could do was wait.

When help finally arrived, the rescuers were equipped with nothing but their bare hands and iron-willed resolve. They pried the metal back, piece by piece, wedging themselves into the wreckage. Without hydraulic tools, every movement was slow and brutal, but they didn't stop. It was sheer willpower that finally freed her, inch by painful inch, pulling her from the mangled metal that could have become her grave.

Nearly two months later, Ida lies in a sunlit room at the Superhumans medical facility in Lviv. The walls are sterile white, still carrying the smell of fresh paint. Outside her window, the world moves on. In this new facility, time moves differently. In the hallway, new amputees wheel themselves with grim faces, eyes carrying the shock of recent loss, every movement a reminder of what's gone. Their hands clutch the sides of their wheelchairs, white-knuckled, navigating this new reality one careful push at a time.

Those who have been here longer take cautious, uneven steps, wobbling slightly as they test their new prosthetics. Their loved ones walk beside them, hands ready to catch a stumble. Each step is an act of faith, trusting that the artificial legs will hold, that they won't betray them. Every shift in balance comes with a glance to the side, seeking reassurance in the calm steadiness of a partner's hand.

On the first floor, some of the residents who have accepted their fate—embraced it—wear a quiet defiance. They laugh, challenging each other to a game of ping pong. The rhythmic sound of the ball pinging back and forth cuts through the silence. There are smiles, real smiles—proof that life, however changed, can still find its way through.

Ida sits alone in her bed, her left leg ending in a neatly wrapped stump that feels foreign, something that belongs to another body. Her burned hand has recovered. Each morning, she stretches her fingers, willing them back to life. Her right leg is bandaged high. A stain of blood seeps through, a reminder and a warning. The doctors are not sure if they can save it. They might have to take that one, too.

The door opens, and a nurse enters with a tray. Ida watches her set down the food without a word. It's routine, sterile—another piece of her new life.

I sit at her bedside, in the only chair available—her wheelchair. Ida's young face, framed by long brown dreads, is almost happy, calm, like a kid home with the flu. I feel an ache rise in my chest. She's so young. She could be my granddaughter. I have to swallow hard, fighting the urge to tear up. My translator, Lera, sensing my struggle, whispers a few words of comfort, a gentle reminder to stay strong. But who am I to need comfort?

During our conversation, she gives me a glimpse into how her mind works. "Anything you cannot control, there is no point in worrying about it. If something happens to you, don't get angry. Fix it. Go forward. Figure out a solution."

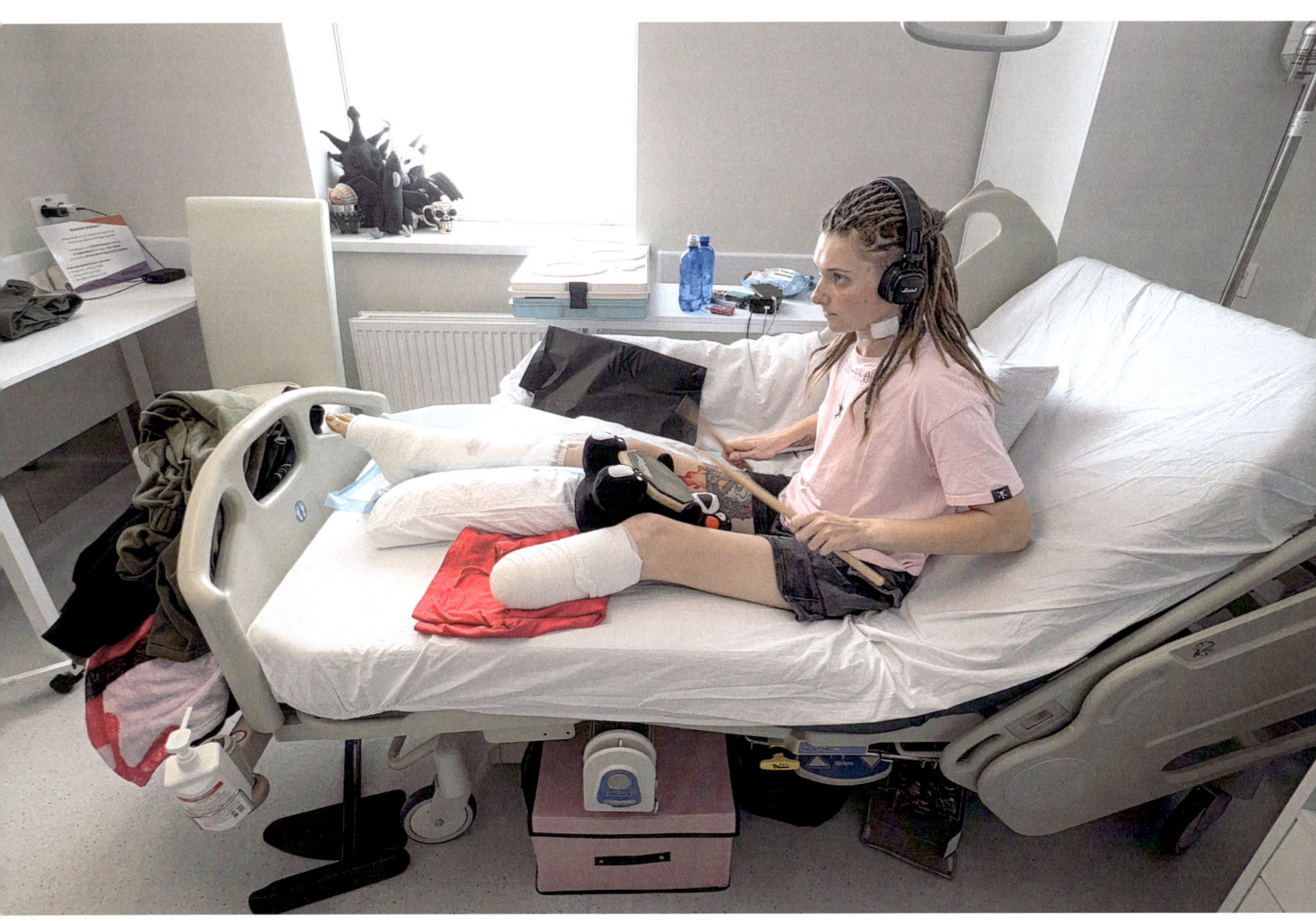

Ida shifts in bed, reaching into the bedside drawer, and pulls out a pair of new wooden drumsticks. She wedges a small drum pad between her bare thighs, then slips on her headset and begins to drum. Her hands are hesitant at first, her brow creased as she stumbles over the rhythm. She stops, closes her eyes, and takes a slow breath. Then she begins again, and this time, there's a spark. The sticks bounce with a steady rhythm. Her head starts to rock. Her eyes close.

She is lost in the beat, which seems to take her away. Somewhere else. She's on stage, bathed in light, a thousand voices cheering her name. Her bandmates play behind her, but she's the one they're all watching, their eyes fixed on her energy, her passion. The crowd is on their feet, roaring, every beat of her drum pulling them into her world.

And in this hospital room, she's drumming on, lost in the rhythm, lost in her strength, refusing to let go.

The Story of a POW: Kateryna – Bird of Steel

It's a blustery fall afternoon in Kyiv. Outside, the wind scatters leaves across the sidewalk, each swirl carrying an undercurrent of tension that seems to mirror the city itself. My translator and I are upstairs in a small restaurant, waiting. Kateryna arrives—stout and sturdy, with a warm smile that contrasts with the military pants she's wearing. Beside her is a man in his thirties, introduced as Maxim. When they sit down, there's a quiet authority about Maxim, an air of command that suggests he's more than just her companion. I notice the black Beretta holstered at his hip. Is he her bodyguard? Or perhaps here in Ukraine, people like Kateryna leave nothing to chance.

By the age of 13, Kateryna already knew her calling—she was born to be an EMT, born to defend her country. Her studies directed her toward a different dream: she wanted to be an opera singer. But when Russia seized Crimea, her purpose sharpened into something she could never have imagined.

In 2021, Kateryna Polishchuk—known by her military call sign "Ptashka," or "bird"—joined the National Guard as a volunteer paramedic. At just 20, as fighting escalated in Mariupol, she lost her boyfriend to the Russians as he frantically searched for her. His body was never returned to Ukraine. Haunted by the loss, Kateryna returned to Mariupol to lend her skills in his memory. Now, at 23, she carries more scars than most.

Mariupol, a once-beautiful city in southeastern Ukraine, was home to the sprawling Azovstal steel plant—a fortress and factory in one.

When Soviet planners rebuilt Azovstal in the 1940s, they began with the bomb shelters, embedding a fortified network deep beneath the steel mill. These bunkers, built to withstand wartime conditions, weren't merely for shelter; they were designed to keep production running under siege—a contingency against both Western and Soviet threats. For Mariupol's residents, Azovstal's bunkers—the only real ones in town—were a relic of civil defense drills and a remembered lifeline. Stretching over four miles, this maze of more than 30 bunkers and tunnels was built to withstand heavy bombardment—a true Soviet-era "fortress."

In April 2022, as Russian forces closed in, Azovstal became the heart of a desperate last stand, the final bastion against an encroaching enemy. Kateryna was deep underground. The bunkers and tunnels of Azovstal shook under relentless Russian bombardment. In the dim glow of flashlights and lamps powered by car batteries, hundreds of civilians and Ukrainian fighters huddled against damp concrete walls. Live electrical wires dangled overhead like frayed nerves, while water and oil pooled in the corners, seeping through cracks; it was a place of survival eroded by war.

The Women of Ukraine 74

Kateryna pushed through with a knee wound and a partially paralyzed arm, refusing to let her injuries stop her. Sleep was scarce; many lay on benches cushioned only by the worn uniforms of steel plant workers. For Kateryna, this was the last chance to save the women, children, and wounded defenders trapped in Azovstal. She worked tirelessly, occasionally performing surgery without anesthesia on wounded soldiers as others succumbed one by one. First aid supplies dwindled to almost nothing, and clean water became a memory. Around her, the defenders fought for days on end, going three or four days without sleep or food. The shelling continued through the nights, as ceilings and walls began to crumble. Yet Kateryna pressed on. Her determination became a lifeline against the fading hope around her. Ptashka—the Bird, kept moving through the shadows, bearing the weight of survival.

For toilets, they had only buckets. When the shelling intensified and it became too dangerous to empty them outside, they resorted to plastic bags that piled up in the cramped, suffocating spaces. The stench became part of the air they breathed, mingling with mold and military hardware—a constant reminder of their confinement. Every task, once simple, became an act of survival, each decision balanced between necessity and the brutal reality of the bombardment above.

In mid-May 2022, the order came from the Ukrainian General Staff: the Azov Battalion was to surrender. For Kateryna and the others, it was a bitter pill. "We knew that as long as Azovstal stood, as long as Russia poured most of its military force into Mariupol, it made it easier for our brothers to fight across Ukraine." They also knew that staying meant that more would die, yet leaving felt like abandoning the fight. She pauses as she tells me this, her gaze steady, the weight of it all etched in her face. Then she adds, "For the Russians, killing comes easier than sipping their coffee."

Kateryna lifts her coffee cup to emphasize her point. When I ask about the moment of surrender, she places it back on the saucer, her gaze dropping. "This is always scary for me to talk about."

She explains that she entered the bunkers in the dead of winter, only to emerge months later into a transformed world. It was early morning, the landscape charred and smeared in shades of black and gray—a springtime stripped of life. Rain fell softly, mingling with ash, blurring the ruins around them.

"Before we were captured, we were told to destroy our phones—to leave no trace of anything important." Kateryna's voice tightens as she recalls it. "I saved what I could, transferring memories onto a flash drive: songs I loved, photos of friends, moments with those who didn't make it. My history, all that I couldn't bear to lose." She pauses, a flicker of resolve in her eyes. "I hid the drive in my shoe."

As they walked toward the enemy's buses, Russian soldiers lined the path, heckling and jeering, their shouts dripping with contempt. "You will die!" they screamed. "You are nothing. You are shit." The words struck like stones, stripping away whatever dignity the Ukrainians still clung to.

Ptashka—the Bird—was about to be caged.

The soldiers searched them, ripping away jewelry, medicine, even essential items like insulin. "We'll give them back," they sneered—a hollow promise, a lie that hung in the air as they boarded, knowing they'd never see those items again. Miraculously, they missed the thumb drive.

The Russian soldiers herded them onto city buses commandeered from Mariupol, shoving them into cramped seats under a barrage of insults. The buses lurched forward, winding through the gutted remains of the city. Through the windows, they saw makeshift graves lining the streets—raw mounds of earth and crude markers standing as silent witnesses to those left behind. The ruins of Mariupol blurred past, a grim reminder of all they had lost, as the buses carried them deeper into the unknown.

Over the next four months, Kateryna was transferred through three different Russian prisons.

She describes the cells: cement rooms reinforced with steel bars, never meant to hold so many. "If a room was built for two, they'd pack in a dozen. If it was built for six, they crammed in 35." In her cell, designed for six, 29 prisoners huddled together on the cold, rough concrete floor. A single hole in the corner served as their toilet, a crude reminder of their dehumanization.

Sometimes, the guards would toss in three one-liter bottles of river water—barely enough to meet even their most basic needs. They used it for everything: drinking, cleaning, bathing, even flushing the pit. In Donetsk, during the stifling summer months, conditions grew even worse. Each prisoner was rationed a single glass—60 milliliters of water a day, just enough to keep them alive.

Occasionally, at one prison, Kateryna and the others were allowed outside to work or bake bread—a brief respite from relentless confinement. But interrogations came regularly, a ritual of rubber batons, humiliation, and torture. Kateryna saw men and women beaten to death, their bodies dragged away as chilling reminders of the cost of resistance. "During any interrogation," she tells me, her voice steady, "you can't spit in the general's face. You have to be smarter."

Kateryna lived each day knowing she could be killed at any moment, but to her, the thought of giving up was worse than death itself. Her hope never wavered; she clung to the knowledge that her country needed her strength. "It's not scary to die," she insists, her eyes fierce. "It's scary to give up."

"The Red Cross in Russia is a piece of shit," Kateryna says bluntly. "They were supposed to meet us when we arrived, but no one ever came. The Red Cross didn't do what they promised. In Russia, their focus is on money, not saving lives. It's a big difference from the Red Cross in Ukraine, where they actually look after Russian captives."

In prison, Kateryna tells me, her fellow prisoners were "treated worse than pigs. The food, if any, was so bad it could hardly be called food." Yet even the smallest scraps, no matter how vile, became a reason to celebrate.

One day, when the guards delivered bottles of murky river water, Kateryna and her cellmates noticed a tiny tadpole swimming inside. They quickly adopted it, naming it "Halia." They fed their unlikely companion crumbs from their meager bread rations. Occasionally, a mouse from another cell would scurry in as a guest, a tiny visitor they named "Larissa."

By the end of the week, as Halia the tadpole swam peacefully in its bottle, a prisoner who shared the same name took offense, feeling mocked by the comparison. With a huff, she tossed the tadpole into the toilet hole. Reactions in the cell were mixed—some cheered, others protested, and for a brief moment, laughter and spirited arguments filled the cramped space, a rare taste of normalcy in an otherwise unforgiving world.

When Kateryna first heard she'd be freed in a prisoner swap, she didn't believe it. She was certain it was just another lie, convinced they were moving her to yet another prison. She and the others were shuffled from buses to planes—two flights in total, with a stopover in Moscow to pick up another prisoner—before finally boarding a second plane to Belarus. Her eyes were covered by a black hood, her hands bound. During the flights, guards walked the aisles, randomly tasering them without warning.

After two days in transit, they were back on a bus. There was no toilet, just endless hours of waiting and uncertainty.

The moment she realized freedom was close came when the bus slowed to a halt and she heard voices speaking Ukrainian.

Kateryna stepped off the bus onto her homeland's soil. The freed prisoners were welcomed with double-decker buses, ambulances for the injured, and smiling Ukrainian officers waiting with bags of gifts. The Russians they'd been exchanged for were loaded onto the same grimy Russian buses that had brought the Ukrainians, to be shuttled back into Russia.

On September 21st, after 125 days in captivity, Kateryna stood on the soil of the country she loves. Her plans were already clear. "I need to get back to the front line," she said, her resolve unshaken.

She takes another sip of her coffee, leans in, and tells me, "I will fight for my country until this war is over."

Kateryna's story sinks in deeply, and I find myself trying to piece it all together.

I'm not entirely sure what her relationship is with Maxim, so I ask. In response, she leans in and gives him a quick kiss. They both laugh, and I capture the moment with my phone.

Maxim tells me that when they first met, she was in a hospital rehabilitation center. "I knew right away she could do anything," he says, glancing at her with admiration. When I ask what he likes most about her, she playfully reaches for his pistol, already anticipating his response. Laughing, he says, "I love looking into her eyes. I love her smile. With her, anything is possible."

Maxim is a battalion commander. The worn leather holster of his black Beretta pistol looks as though it's a part of his hip. He commands 500 defenders, leading them into battle and on combat missions. Among them are 10 women: some are doctors, others drone pilots. "We need more drones. In one month alone, we lost 100 Mavics," he says, his eyes locking onto mine to drive the point home. "Even if I lose an arm or a leg, I'll still be alive, with a life worth living. We're fighting for our very existence. The Russians want nothing less than to destroy us."

I tell him, "I brought some donations from American friends. If I gave you $500, what would you use it for?" Without missing a beat, he replies, "Antennas for our drones. You can't imagine how many Russians you can take out with a Mavic 3. It can carry up to 700 grams of explosives."

Maxim holds out his phone, eagerly to make his point. A black-and-white aerial video flickers on the cracked screen, capturing the sudden flash of an explosion, then the final moments of a Russian soldier, sprawled and dying on the ground.

The waitress brings me another cappuccino. Kateryna's smile has faded. She looks at me, her voice quiet but firm. "I need to tell you... a minute ago, when you took that photo, it triggered some flashbacks. During interrogations, the Russians would take photos of us." She pauses, letting it sink in. "Next time, please ask. Give me some warning."

A wave of guilt hits me. I'm uncomfortably reminded of my own ignorance, how removed I am from the brutal realities she's endured. But then, with a gentle shrug, her smile returns—understanding, forgiving. She lets me off the hook, her strength softened with compassion.

When I ask what message she'd like to share with Americans, Kateryna pauses, her gaze steady. "I would remind them that no amount of money is worth the life and peace of your children. I hope Americans' children never experience what our country is going through. We have to stop Russia now. If we don't, it will continue, on and on… No one needs to build connections with Russia. As we know, they'll stick a knife in you at any moment." She offers a faint smile and adds, "Give us the opportunity to save the world from Russia."

Moments later, the waitress is back, this time thanking them for their courage and saying that the manager wishes to cover their meal—a small gesture of gratitude for sacrifices beyond words.

By 8 p.m., Maxim and Ptashka are back on the front lines. The Bird has come home, her wings tested by war, but unbroken.

The Women of Ukraine   78

Brushstrokes of Loss

In a quiet corner of a small library in Lviv, Iryna paints alongside a community of women, all bound by loss. Each brushstroke tells a story, one of grief and resilience. These women have lost husbands, sons, and daughters, yet – here together – they create something beautiful out of their pain.

Iryna's husband, Volodymyr, was 54 when he died. He had been missing for a year before they found him. "I'm joining the army to protect my wife and my country," he had said before leaving. He never came back.

In her painting, shades of deep blue and soft white blend to form a winter scene. The branches of a bare tree stretch across the canvas, and in the distance is their family home site...a small red refuge beneath the vast sky. Volodymyr's hands, though absent, seem to cradle the home, as if still watching over it. The colors swirl with quiet strength, capturing the love and protection he left behind.

Asked why she paints, Iryna doesn't hesitate: "The most important thing is preserving the memory for all our people...so the whole world knows what a price we have paid and the pain we have endured."

This act of painting, alongside other women who share her grief, has become Iryna's way of keeping him close. Through her art, she preserves not only Volodymyr's memory but the legacy of countless others.

Victoria's hands don't shake as she gently brushes brown strokes of paint into her son's hair.

"He was 25 when he was killed. The first time he ever drove was with his unit in the war. They just told him, 'Get in and drive!' This painting is from a photo he sent me. He was laughing, saying, 'When I get home, I'm going to get my driver's license!' He was so excited."

She pauses, looking at her work. "I love this picture because he looks so happy."

Yesterday would have been his birthday. He died in 2023, in a place called the Silver Forest.

Two Lovebirds and One Lonely Sparrow

The streets of Lviv are full of stories…and awkward bench moments. Sometimes love is just too much, especially when it's not yours. On one side, a couple is wrapped in their own world, oblivious to the chill in the air. On the other, a man sits hunched, staring at the ground, as if wondering why fate put him on *this* bench at *this* moment.

In a war-torn city, even the awkward moments hold a story waiting to be told.

Caged Statues

Walking through the heart of Lviv, I see a city ready to protect its soul. Statues, wrapped and caged, stand tall, like silent sentinels, while church windows are often boarded up, shielding the history and culture that the invading Russians are trying to erase. The streets, though quiet for now, have an underlying tension that reminds everyone this struggle is far from over. But in this act of preservation, there's also defiance. You can cover the monuments, but you'll never crush the spirit behind them.

War's Lingering Reach

The air raid sirens have become a haunting rhythm, a constant reminder of war's reach. In a Soviet-era bunker, a young woman focuses on her studies, her laptop casting a glow against the cold, gray walls. Nearby, a rusted gas mask and an obsolete telephone communication system sit abandoned, relics of another era when war was on the horizon. These remnants of the past share space with the stark realities of today, bridging generations through the unyielding shadow of conflict. Above ground, a mother and her child seek fragile refuge. The mother's eyes often dart skyward at the sound of the sirens, a reflex born from the trauma of fleeing their village as bombs shattered their home. Here, survival is not just enduring the war but weaving together fragments of normalcy stolen from the pervading chaos, even as the bunker's history serves as a solemn reminder that war, in all its forms, persists.

If there's a common thread I have found during my time in Ukraine, a land shaken daily by war, it's the quiet defiance of gripping onto a sense of control amid the chaos—a determination throughout the country to reclaim even the smallest pieces of life that cannot be dictated by bombs or Putin's decisions.

A father and daughter glide along a deserted railway platform in Moronovka, the child perched confidently on the bike with her hands steady, as though guiding herself into a future yet unwritten. Far away in Lviv, a woman has transformed her longing for her homeland into a small act of resistance: a Crimean café, where the scent of home-cooked Croatian cabbage rolls drifts around her patrons like a comforting embrace. In a gym, defenders practice wrestling techniques, ready to return to the front. And then there's the tattoo artist, her dark silhouette framed by weathered wooden doors, her artistry etched on the skin of heroes and waiting lovers, immortalizing beauty and rebellion in equal measure.

Together, they refuse to let this war dictate who they are or how they choose to endure.

The Silence Between Us

Two bright red chairs sit beneath the dappled shade of a tree, their metal legs anchored on the uneven paving stones of a quiet courtyard. Though empty, the space between them is heavy, not with absence, but with all that could be said...and all that has been lost.

The war has stolen so much: words, lives, futures. Yet here, in this small corner of a battered city, the chairs seem to resist the silence. They face each other as if pleading for a truce, a place to start again. Their quiet persistence feels like a metaphor; a fragile hope that even in devastation, there might still be room for dialogue, for healing.

Above them, the branches sway in rhythm with the wind, whispering secrets only trees understand. Perhaps they remember the voices of those who once sat here—parents negotiating their children's futures, lovers dreaming aloud, strangers finding solace in a fleeting conversation. The pigeon that pecks nearby doesn't notice, or doesn't care, how significant this meeting place has become.

The chairs are more than furniture now. They are witnesses to what remains. They hold the weight of unsaid apologies, shattered dreams, and the stubborn resilience of people who keep going. They face each other, not in defiance, but in quiet determination. They seem to beg: Sit, share, unburden. Speak of what the war took, of what it didn't, of what still might be.

This courtyard is no longer a place for laughter alone—it is a stage for reckoning. These chairs silently demand honesty, the kind that aches and heals all at once. They are waiting for someone brave enough to sit, to mourn, to hope.

For now, the chairs wait, like all of us; patient, burdened, but refusing to yield.

Coffee with Jesus

It's 7 a.m. on a Monday, and the summer sun is just beginning to warm the cobblestones of Lviv's city center. I've settled on a weathered bench, nursing a cup of strong Americano, the steam rising in lazy spirals like incense in a Catholic church. The square is still quiet, save for the occasional clatter of tram wheels and the soft murmur of early commuters.

Across the square, a timeworn wooden cross stands in solemn silence, darkened and splintered—a quiet testament to years of sorrow and hope. Jesus looks down, suspended above in silent despair.

A woman balances a bag of vegetables as she boards a tram; a boy tugs at his mother's hand, eager to chase a pigeon. The square begins to stir, but here at the cross, time seems to still itself.

Teens hurry past, cell phones buzzing, perhaps holding onto more hope than the darkened skies over Ukraine seem to allow. Others cross themselves and continue on their way. Some pause, their eyes darting nervously as they glance upward at the figure of Christ before approaching the towering cross.

Gray-haired men and women, their shoulders stooped, are the ones who most often stop and look up, their faces etched with the strain of living through another war. One by one, they hesitate, as if unsure whether to intrude on this sacred space. Yet almost inevitably, they are drawn in, as though compelled by some invisible force. Their hands rest at their sides, their feet together in a stance of quiet respect. Their lips move in silent conversation, their heads tilting up as if asking, "Why?"

When the silent exchange ends, they press their foreheads against a well-worn spot on the wood and cross themselves one more time.

I watch as an old man, his hands trembling, wraps his arms around the base of the cross, embracing it. He rests his head against it, his eyes closed. In that moment, two figures seem to hang on the cross. He stays like that, letting the steadfast presence of the cross anchor him.

Later, an older woman dressed in black, as if in mourning, crosses herself and whispers, as though searching for a prayer she can no longer voice. Finally, she steps forward, her fingers grazing the rough wood. She gently presses her lips to it, lingering for a moment—perhaps hoping to draw strength from it, or perhaps to leave behind a part of her burden to rest alongside the countless others it holds.

It is a simple daily ritual—a brief, quiet communion that seems to offer the reassurance Ukrainians so desperately need amid the chaos of a country standing defiant against Putin's relentless invasion.

As Jesus looks down, a blond woman quietly kisses the cross. I take another sip of my coffee, the bitterness mingling with the bittersweet sight before me...a reminder that in the midst of war and despair, faith remains unshaken, like the cross itself—a source of fragile grace.

In an old Ukrainian estate, once abandoned, life echoes again—a refuge for women and children who fled as Russian artillery destroyed their homes. This spiral staircase now hears the laughter of children who've seen too much for their age. These two kids play with a donated bike, their fragile innocence spinning upward despite the horrors below. Even when the world crumbles, hope finds its footing.

The Fabric of Loss

On a bustling street corner in the heart of Kyiv…a quiet memorial grows: a sea of blue and yellow flags fluttering softly in the breeze. Each flag bears the name of a fallen soldier, a life cut short by war. Behind every flag lies a story: a love ended too soon, a father who won't come home, a brother or sister never to smile again. Here, in this corner of the city, time feels suspended. The world rushes on, but this small patch of earth holds its breath.

A woman kneels down, her delicate hand reaching to plant another flag. Her nails—perfectly manicured, polished in soft, muted tones—speak of a life that once knew ordinary joys: laughter, dinners with friends, dancing with her boyfriend. In a world spinning out of control, her carefully kept nails are her last hold on normalcy, a fragile reminder of dignity. She presses the flag into the ground. Her fingertips brush the fabric as if to hold onto the memory it represents. The name of the love of her life—"Misha Mikheev"—is written there, another thread in the fabric of loss. Beside it, a friend: "Максим Абрамович."

Nearby, among the same solemn rows of flags, another scene unfolds. A mother kneels beside her young son. Together they are surrounded by a sea of color—vibrant flags, flowers, and photos of fallen loved ones. The mother's gaze softens as she meets her son's eyes. Small hands rest in hers as she tries to explain the unexplainable: that his father, like so many others, gave everything for their country.

The boy listens, his face a mixture of tears and questions no child should ever have to ask. His mother whispers words of bravery, sacrifice, and love, though she knows they are far too weighty for his small heart to carry. Still, she holds him close, her embrace a fragile shield against the enormity of their grief.

In both moments—the woman planting a flag and the mother comforting her child—beauty and loss exist side by side. Yet, in their small, tender acts, they refuse to let despair win. The woman's manicured hands and the mother's soft voice are quiet testaments to the human need to hold onto love and dignity, even in the darkest of times.

A light breeze sends a gentle ripple through the flags in their rows, like a silent chorus echoing: "We are still here…"

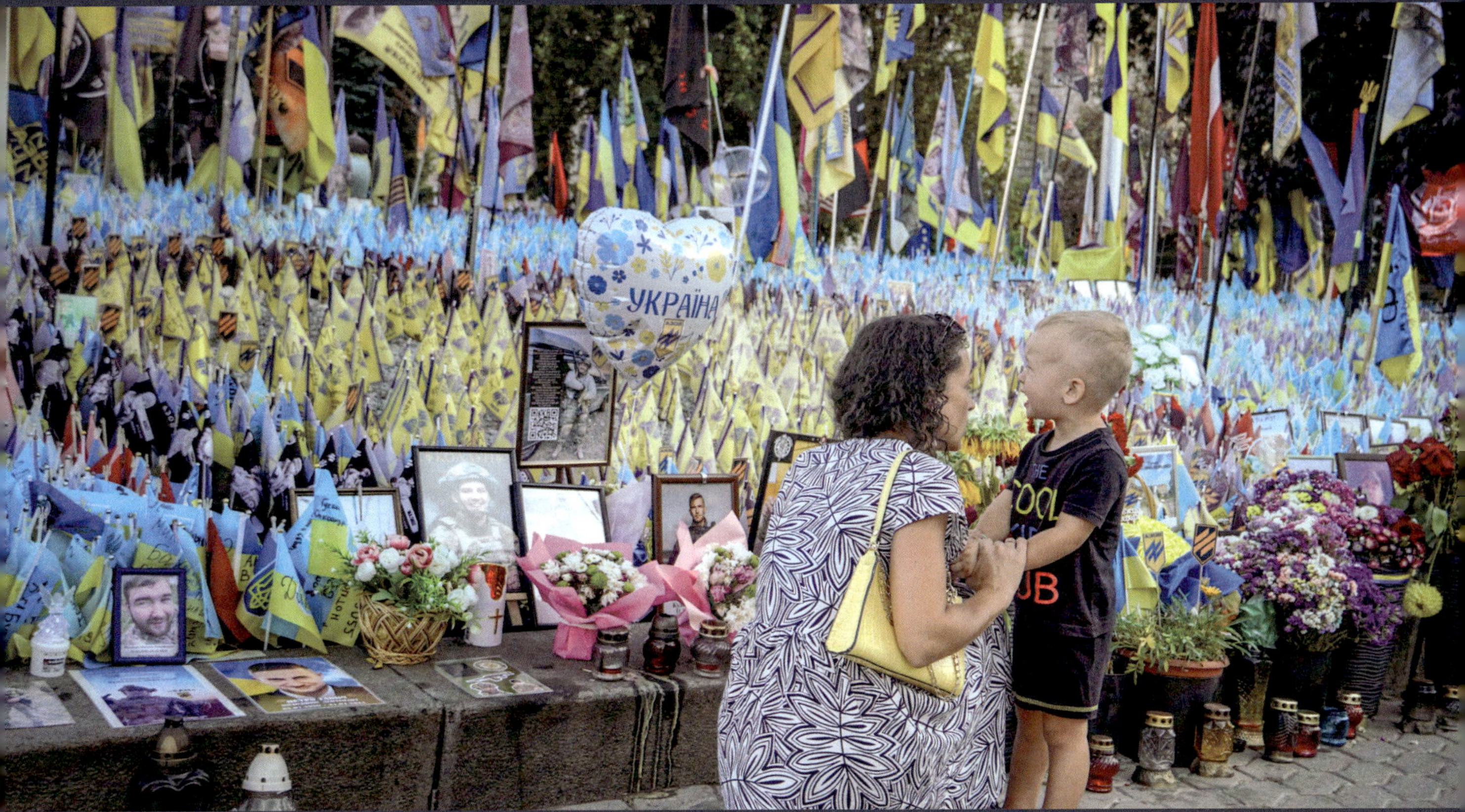
УКРАЇНА

МИХАЙЛО
МІХЕЕВ
МАКСИМ
АБРАМОВИЧ

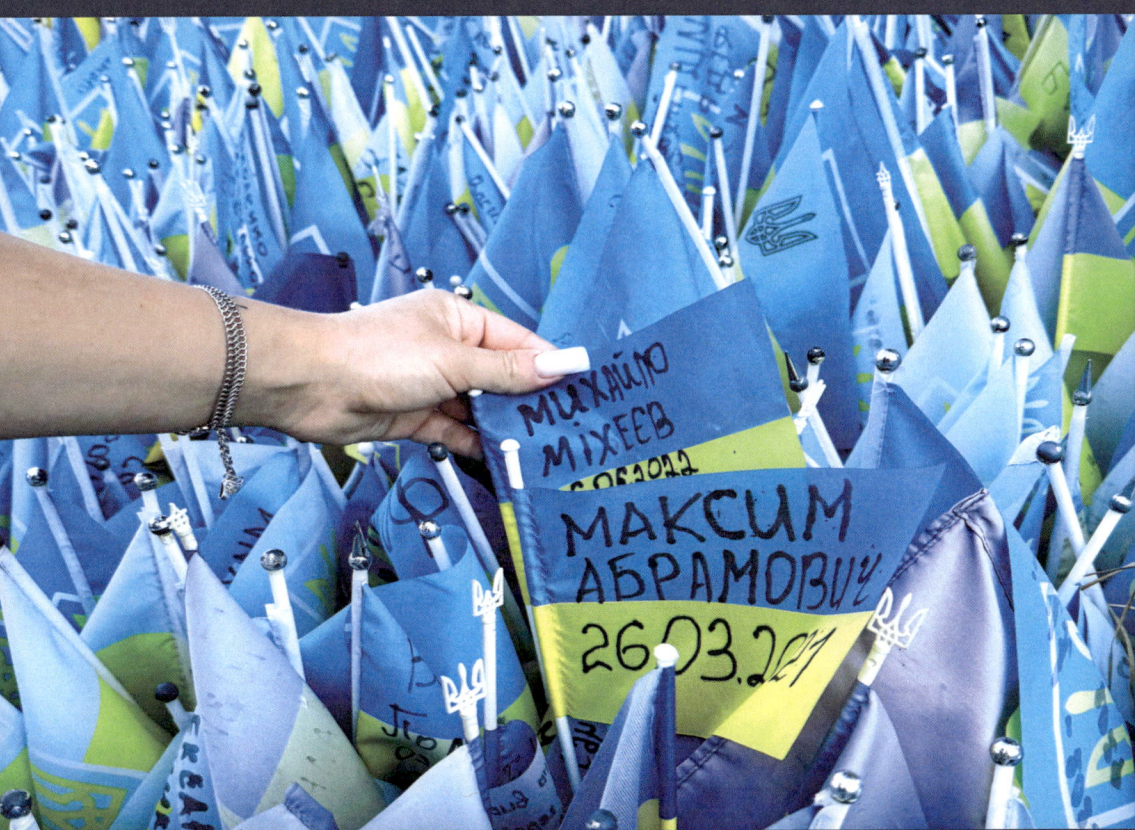

The Price of a View: 19 Flights Down to Safety

The Black Sea whispers to Odesa, but its voice is quieter now, tinged with uncertainty. The vibrant bustle that once defined this port city has given way to an uneasy calm, the sound of waves lapping against a shoreline nearly devoid of life.*

A few locals wander the small beach, their figures swallowed by the vast emptiness. Others stand along seawalls, rusting railings framing the small harbor, their fishing lines trailing into the dark waters. Beyond them, a fragile procession of cargo ships drifts on the horizon, their hulls burdened with Ukrainian grain—and quiet desperation. Each vessel is a gamble, a silent prayer that the Russians won't strike from above.

My feet sink into the beach sand. For a moment, I imagine my son and me sailing out there on his white hulled boat, chasing ripples of wind on the water. But the vision shatters as I spot the caution sign: "Warning: Floating Mines." Every wave conceals its own threat.

In the sprawling marketplace, survival clings stubbornly to routine. The air hangs heavy with the pungent gamey smell of raw beef and the weight of time slipping away. Older women sit behind counters piled high with unrefrigerated meat, their weathered arms—pork-like and strong from years of butchering—resting on stained tabletops. Chins perch on hands, their gazes anchored in quiet endurance. Each face looks like a relic from another era, belonging to a character in a forgotten Russian novel. I ache to capture their portraits in a single frame.

I approach the first babushka. I'm careful to keep my camera stowed in my sling bag. The iPhone will be enough and it's always unobtrusive. My request is shot down with the precision of a missile. No smile, no hesitation—just a firm, unyielding *nyet*, with the punctuating sweep of her arm, dispersing the flies.

In Ukrainian, the city's name is spelled Odesa with one "s," reflecting the correct Ukrainian form (Одеса). The spelling Odessa with two "s"s comes from the Russian version of the name.

The Women of Ukraine 96

I spot another face, round and creased with time. My translator and I pause to strategize. We approach with care, first asking about the beef. The woman's eyes flicker with a hint of light as she explains that she and her husband raised the cows on their farm not far from town. I ask more questions, about her family, layering trust. When she tells me about her grandkids, I feel the connection building, as though we're almost friends. Surely, I think, she'll allow one quick photo of her sitting behind the slabs of beef.

There is no need for my translator to relay her response. The sharp tone makes it clear: "No chance in hell." The message is universal, the delivery unmistakable.

I wander into the produce section of the marketplace, a sprawling warehouse packed with tables overflowing with fruits and vegetables. The air is different here: lighter, free from the stench of decaying meat. My eyes scan the vendors until they land on another face to capture with my lens. I lift my camera for a quick shot, but the glare I receive freezes me in place. The message is unmistakable. I lower the camera, tuck it away, and zip my bag shut, feeling the weight of their silent disapproval.

Odesa's vibe is unlike any other place I've visited in Ukraine—a mix of coastal beauty, resilience and refusal, its identity shifting under the weight of war.

The city's skyline tells some of the story. On September 25, 2023, Russian missiles struck Odesa, hitting the iconic Odesa Hotel at the port. Empty since 2011, the building sustained significant damage, but no lives were lost. The attack wasn't just against a structure; it was an assault on a symbol of the city's soul.

Even the newer hotels look hollow. Their rooms, once vibrating with the cacophony of tourists, now echo with silence. My own hotel greets me with a grimly practical sign by the elevator: "In case of air raid alert, go to hideout. Take care of yourself so we can celebrate victory." A fragile thread of hope stitched into the fabric of war.

I thought I'd chosen my room wisely—nineteen floors up, an unobstructed view of Odesa stretching to the sea. But when the first air raid sirens pierce the dawn, I realize my mistake. Nineteen flights of stairs. At 73, I weigh my odds: Will I trip halfway down and tear open my knee? Or will an incoming missile send me straight to the basement? The sirens' wail reverberates through the hollow hallways.

Many of the Shahed drones and missiles are launched from Russian warships near Crimea, making Odesa an easy target in the first line of fire. Outside, Ukrainian defenders take a fragile stand against the chaos, tracking the nighttime skies with unwavering focus.

Streaks of light carve through the darkness in a silent choreography of danger and defiance as tracer missiles claw upward with arcs that are fleeting—momentary bursts of hope trying to stave off destruction.

I roll over in bed and close my eyes.

When the sirens finally fade, silence takes their place. For me, it's heavy, uneasy, and full of questions. In Odesa, every room with a beautiful view comes with a steep price that is always shadowed by the weight of escape. I can't help but hope that one day, it will offer more than survival.

The Women of Ukraine 98

They Killed You, But You Never Left

In the quiet corners of Ukraine, love whispers goodnight to an empty pillow

She makes two cups of coffee every morning.
One for her.
One for him.

The second cup goes untouched, placed on the bench beside the grave, just like always. It's become less a ritual, more a conversation.

At night, her hand finds the hollow of the pillow he used to sleep on. The dent is still there, holding its shape like a refusal to forget.

She texts him goodnight.
Same words. Same time.
The screen stays dark, but she does it anyway.

Sometimes she whispers lullabies into the silence, the way she did when he came home shaking.

Her wedding ring stays warm, strung around her neck, resting just above her heartbeat. He said once that her pulse calmed him. She hopes it still does.

His last shirt still smells like him. She folds it slow, then folds it again. She doesn't put it away.

The baby kicks, a little harder each day.
She presses her hand to her belly and asks the room,
"Did you feel that, love?"

The porch light stays on, even when the blackout rolls in.
Habit.
Hope.
Maybe both.

His toothbrush still leans against the wall, stiff with dust.
She hasn't moved it. Won't.

She wears his jacket when the nights get cold.
Not because she's cold.
Because the sleeves still know how to hold her.

But he's still there, in ways she can feel.
This is what he might've said, if he'd had one more minute.

My Love,

If I could, I'd start with the small things.
Tell you to stop making me coffee—I never liked it black.
But I'd drink it anyway, if it meant five more minutes with you.

I'd ask if the pillow still smells like us.
If you still fall asleep to the sound of that one lullaby, the one you hummed
without knowing you were doing it.

I'd tell you I saw you fold my shirt.
How you paused halfway, pressed it to your face.
I wanted to reach out. Say nothing. Just… be there.

Is it true? Is there really a baby now?
Did we make something that keeps growing
even when I don't?

I'd give anything to feel your hand on your belly.
To say, Yes, love. I felt it too.

And the porch light—
God, I saw it.
Flickering like you were fighting the dark with everything you had.
You always did.

I miss the smell of your skin in my jacket.
The way you'd steal it like it was yours.
(It was.)

I wish I could touch your hair,
still wet from the shower, tangled at the ends.
Kiss your shoulder.
Tell you the war didn't win.

But I can't.
So instead, I wait.
Here.
In the smell of that last shirt.
In the dust on my toothbrush.
In the second cup of coffee that always goes cold.

I'm still yours.
Even now.

—Me

She still makes two cups. He still shows up.

The war has stolen much from Ukraine—lives, homes, and a sense of normalcy. But here, amidst the pain and loss, Unbroken represents the resilience of a nation and the extraordinary women like Roxalana who help carry it forward.

Unbroken: A Hub of Humanity

It's a sunny fall day outside the new buildings of Unbroken--an ecosystem of over twenty interconnected hospital services in Lviv, offering everything from prosthetics and physical therapy to psychological counseling, housing, and reintegration support.

Roxalana Shmylo, a physical therapist with a steady gaze and the kind of calm earned through years of caring for others, watches her patient, 30-year-old Olexee, navigate the long path of gravel on his prosthetic leg.

"That's it," she calls out encouragingly, her voice a blend of authority and warmth. Olexee focuses on the task at hand, as he moves to the next challenge: a precarious walkway of small logs. His steps are hesitant but determined. Sitting on a nearby bench, his wife, Anistatinan, 31, shifts slightly in the autumn sunlight. Her eyes are locked on her husband's every move, her expression a mix of pride and love.

"When he was fighting on the front, I started to worry when he didn't answer his phone," she shares, her voice soft but steady. "His commander called me late one evening with the horrible news. During the next several days, I worried constantly, not just about him but about what our life would be like now that he had lost his leg. When I rushed through the hospital doors, I didn't know what to say. Should I talk about relatives? About the weather? Should I ignore the gravity of it all?"
She pauses, a smile breaking through the memory. "And then, in just a few moments, he made me laugh, like he always does. I knew, somehow, things were going to be okay."

Unbroken is aptly named for the spirit it cultivates. The atmosphere inside is as heavy as it is inspiring. A steady stream of legless and armless patients drifts like ghosts past one another in the halls. Some wear faint smiles of Ukrainian optimism; others bear a haunting stare that speaks of horrors they cannot forget.

Since the invasion, more than 19,000 wounded Ukrainians—children among them—have sought treatment at Unbroken. The center is more than just a hospital. It's a humanitarian hub–a symbol of the country's resilience.

This is where Roxalana thrives. Her office wall displays a list of more than 1,000 patients she's treated. Many still send her photos, call her from the front lines, or text her updates. "More than 60% of my patients go back to the front," she says, a mix of pride and sadness in her voice. "For many, after being in the war, civilian life is not for them."

Roxalana isn't just a physical therapist. She's part psychologist, part advocate, and part organizer—a lifeline for her patients in their darkest moments. "Each one of their stories is a part of my heart," she says.

The work is painstaking. Every new patient undergoes a comprehensive consultation with a multidisciplinary team, including rehabilitation medicine specialists, prosthetists, physiotherapists, psychotherapists, and, if needed, surgeons and traumatologists. "We all examine the patient," Roxalana explains. "Then I design a personalized rehabilitation program."

Rehabilitation isn't just about physical recovery; it's about teaching a new way of life. For patients with upper-limb amputations, the process involves mastering fine motor skills and adapting prosthetics for daily tasks like tying shoelaces or cooking. For those with leg amputations, it means learning to walk again, first with crutches, then with a prosthetic.

Outside, Olexee finishes the log walkway, his steps more confident. Anistatinan stands to greet him, her face beaming with pride. "You're amazing," she says softly, her words wrapping around him like a warm embrace.

Roxalana watches the exchange with a small smile. "This is why we do it," she says, almost to herself.

Adrift Through the Ice, a Mother's Impossible Choice

Olena greets me at the door of her ground-floor apartment with a smile that feels like a bright light. As she makes coffee, I sit at a small table in the living room, watching. Olena is eager to share her story. Two of her disabled children wiggle on the floor, giggling softly, while her husband and teenage daughter quietly care for them. The modest room is a mosaic of resilience, marked by colorful balloons in one corner and soft blankets in another—a fragile refuge from a life torn apart by war.

In the early hours of February 24, 2022, the quiet rhythm of Olena and Serhii's farm shattered under the distant roar of explosions. By dawn, the life they had built in the Kherson region—on one of the largest and most successful pig farms in southern Ukraine, feeding thousands of families with pork from their 42,000 pigs—was gone. The Russians were closing in, and escape wasn't just urgent; it was a gamble with death.

Olena was the family's 'steel soldier,' the one who held everything together. Her husband, Serhii, had poured his heart into the farm, even traveling to the United States to learn from American farmers. But no amount of preparation could have readied them for what lay ahead. "On February 24, our life started over, with just one bag," Olena remembers. "We had no choice."

Of their five children, the twin boys, aged eight, had disabilities. Their eldest, a 17-year-old, was autistic and paralyzed. As Russian troops seized control of their town in the strategically vital Kherson region, there was only enough time to pack hurriedly and make the impossible decision to leave their teenage son behind in the care of Olena's mother.

Ukrainian soldiers guided them under fire to the frozen shores of the Dniprovs'ka Gulf. There, they huddled in the biting cold for hours, watching the ice float by, waiting for a small boat to take them across. When the skiff finally arrived, Olena, Serhii, and their four children squeezed into the overcrowded vessel alongside the local mayor's wife and her children. The adults used wooden sticks to break up the ice and push it aside, their breath visible in the freezing air.

"Silence was everything," Olena said. "We turned off our phones and told the children they couldn't make a sound." As the boat drifted through the icy water, they threaded past Russian military ships. The tension was palpable, each stop filling the air with quiet terror. "It was adrenaline that got us through," she said. "I kept thinking, if we're going to die, we must all die together."

Now living in a special-needs residence in Lviv, Olena's family is safe, except for her mother and eldest son, who remain trapped behind enemy lines. Sporadic texts from her mother, sent when she could find a cell signal, revealed the grim reality under Russian occupation. "All the TV channels are gone except the Russian propaganda one that says, 'Ukraine abandoned you,'" her mother wrote. Russian soldiers, often drunk or high, roamed the village. They shot into the air, killed pets, and looted homes.

15 soldiers barged into her house, rifling through everything for valuables. "They took any paper with an official-looking stamp," her mother recounted. "They didn't know all they stole were appliance warranties!" Before leaving, one soldier asked, "What do you think of Russia?" She could only smile faintly and say, "What can one little old woman think?"

For Olena, every day is still a battle with uncertainty. The war stole her farm, scattered her family, and uprooted her life, but it hasn't broken her. As she reflected on their perilous journey, she said, "If I've learned one thing, it's this: no matter how much the Russians take from us, they can't take who we are. We will fight for each other, even when we're apart."

War and Peace: Two Worlds of Fear

In the United States, school shootings have become a tragic reality, with nearly 40 incidents occurring in 2024 alone. The prevalence of gun violence in schools has led to heightened security measures and a pervasive sense of fear among students and parents. Some manufacturers now offer bullet-resistant backpacks made of Kevlar, with removable ballistic panels that can serve as shields in an emergency.

In stark contrast, during my time in Ukraine since the invasion, I observed a different relationship between children and depictions of violence. In Lviv, I met a young boy who proudly showed me his realistic-looking black plastic pistol (no orange-colored tip required). But his favorite toy was a clear plastic grenade filled with yellow bits of candy, all stored in his backpack, ready to take to school. In parks, children and young women pay to "target practice" with BB guns and bows and arrows, aiming at targets depicting the face of Vladimir Putin.

The irony is profound: in a country where war echoes through the nights, children openly carry toy weapons to school and engage in play that mirrors the conflict around them. Yet incidents of actual school shootings are virtually nonexistent. Meanwhile, in the United States, where peace prevails domestically, places of learning have become sites of massacres, where students kill students.

This juxtaposition raises unsettling questions about how societies perceive and manage the presence of weapons and violence in children's lives. In Ukraine, war has so deeply permeated daily life that children incorporate it into their play, perhaps as a means of coping with their reality. In the U.S., despite the absence of a military war, the prevalence of firearms and cultural attitudes toward them have contributed to a tragic epidemic of school shootings.

But Ukrainian children face a different kind of violence. Their schools are not under threat from classmates with guns but from Russian missiles and drones. On May 7, 2022, a Russian airstrike targeted a school in Bilohorivka, Luhansk Oblast, where approximately 90 people had sought shelter. The attack set the building ablaze, trapping many inside, where 60 died.

In response to these threats, cities like Zaporizhzhia have begun constructing underground schools: bomb and radiation-proof structures designed to provide a safe place to learn for thousands of students, many of whom have retreated to online education since the war began.

Despite the absence of school shootings, Ukrainian children remain in constant danger. The contrast is stark: in America, children fear the next armed classmate; in Ukraine, they fear the next air raid siren. Two different worlds, two different nightmares—each shaping a generation in ways we are only beginning to understand.

The sun dips low, casting a golden glow over the village of Huta. Nearby red-roofed farmhouses dot the land, bordered by green fields stretching endlessly. A circular pen stands at the heart of the scene, its wooden fence encasing a lone white mare. She flicks her tail lazily, her coat gleaming in the fading light, while a gentle breeze carries the scent of fresh grass and the faint aroma of blossoming cherry trees. Rows of solar panels glint like polished shields under the sun, a modern touch against a timeless pastoral backdrop. This is a sanctuary of calm amidst a world fractured by war—a fragile paradise at risk of shattering.

Just beyond the farm, the woods begin, their silence broken only by the crunch of dried leaves underfoot and the occasional rustle of a startled bird. A narrow path winds its way through the trees, dappled with light filtering through the spring canopy. The air here is cool and earthy, tinged with the faint metallic tang of recent rain. A fallen log, splintered and weathered, blocks part of the trail, a reminder of the forest's untamed nature. It feels like the kind of place where time slows, where stories can linger like a whisper in the scattered leaves, adding nuance and depth to lives lived in this hidden corner of Ukraine.

From Monaco to the Frontlines: A Plastic Surgeon's Mission to Rebuild Ukraine's Heroes

The first time Oleksandra Mostepan held the shattered remains of a soldier's leg in her hands, she realized her years of sculpting beauty in Monaco had prepared her for something far more profound: rebuilding lives forever changed by war.

Oleksandra's life took an irrevocable turn when war broke out in Ukraine. A renowned plastic and reconstructive surgeon, she had been working in the south of France, perfecting cosmetic procedures in the

glamorous enclaves of Monaco—performing facelifts and breast augmentations. Her career had revolved around enhancing appearances, refining the external. But when Russian forces invaded her homeland, everything shifted.

Her father, a medical doctor, had always instilled in her a deep sense of duty to their country. As Ukraine descended into chaos, Oleksandra knew she couldn't stay away. What once was a pursuit of aesthetics became a mission to save lives and restore the dignity of wounded soldiers. She left the high-end world of cosmetic surgery behind and entered the unforgiving realities of wartime medicine, using her expertise to perform complex reconstructive surgeries. These were no longer about beauty; they were about repairing shattered limbs, mending broken bones, and rebuilding fractured lives.

As a leading figure in her field, Oleksandra quickly became instrumental in the founding of U+ System, a company dedicated to developing cutting-edge prosthetics. The need was both immediate and overwhelming: thousands of soldiers and civilians were returning from the frontlines with life-altering injuries. U+ System emerged as a beacon of hope, providing high-tech solutions to restore functionality, while Oleksandra's leadership and expertise set a new standard for reconstructive surgery during wartime.

Sitting over a cappuccino, Oleksandra speaks candidly about how misunderstood the role of a plastic surgeon often is, especially during a war. In a LinkedIn post, she addressed the discouraging remarks she's heard: "She's a plastic surgeon; what could she possibly do in Ukraine at this time?" To her, such comments miss the point entirely. Plastic and reconstructive surgeons like her are precisely the specialists Ukraine needs—those capable of restoring not just function, but hope. They give soldiers and civilians alike a chance to reclaim a semblance of normalcy after unimaginable trauma.

When she's not in the operating room or leading U+ System, Oleksandra finds solace with her animals. Her horse, Innsbruck, and her tiny dog, Tima, offer her moments of peace amidst the chaos. She recently shared how dressage training, once a lighthearted hobby, has evolved into a vital part of her life. For her, riding is no longer about competition but about trust, harmony, and the healing connection between horse and rider.

As Ukraine endures one of its darkest chapters, Oleksandra's work shines as a testament to resilience. She reminds the world that even amid destruction, there is room for healing—both physical and emotional. For Oleksandra, her homeland is where she is needed most, and she is determined to rebuild, one limb and one life at a time.

111   The Women of Ukraine

Mothers You've Never Heard Of

They are mothers, soldiers, and heroes—women who have taken up arms to defend their homeland. As of September 2024, approximately 68,000 women serve in the Armed Forces of Ukraine, with about 5,000 deployed directly in combat zones. Their commitment challenges traditional gender roles and highlights the evolving role of women in Ukraine's military. Since 2014, the number of women in the Ukrainian military has more than doubled, reflecting a significant shift in societal attitudes and military policy. They're mothers you've never heard of. They are not unlike other moms—they miss their children and proudly share family photos or their kids' artwork. But unlike most moms around the world, they carry AK-47s and are trained defenders, balancing the responsibilities of motherhood with the demands of military service. All of them are ready to fight and, if necessary, lay down their lives for Ukraine.

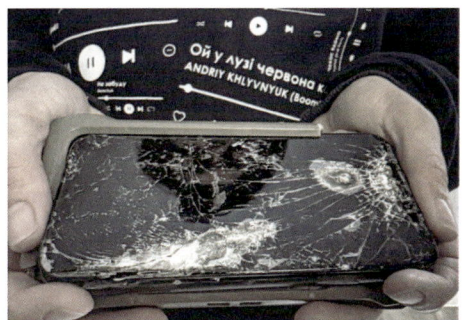

Olena is a mother who dedicates most of her days to supporting Ukraine's defenders. Her only child, a son, enlisted at 20. By 21, he was gone. His bedroom remains untouched—a testament to a life stolen too soon. As she guides me through the space, she picks up his damaged cell phone, remembering their last call. Then his baby photo. Then his rifle, holding it close—her hands moving over the metal as if it were the last piece of him she had left.

What should I tell her about America? That some have moved on, distracted by headlines that shift by the hour? That debates rage over aid while she clings to what remains of her son? Or that there are still those who remember, who care, who refuse to look away?

Every Table Has a Story

The wooden chairs creak, a faint echo in the hushed café. Outside, the streets of Lviv echo with life, the gray sky pressing down on cobblestone streets and the colorful store fronts that brighten their edges. The smell of coffee lingers, mingling with the damp air.

This table has seen it all: whispered confessions between lovers, their knees brushing beneath its scarred surface; the frantic tapping of a journalist's keyboard, racing to capture the latest chronicles from the front; the weight of a soldier's weary elbows, his coffee cooling as he stares out the window, already half-gone to what lies ahead.

A woman's laughter ripples like sunlight breaking through the dusty glass—defiant and alive. In a city of sirens and shadows, laughter is rebellion.

Outside, a smear of red streaks past; a bride in white rushes by, clutching a bundle of roses, their blooms flickering like flames in the muted palette of the city. Beside her is the groom, still dressed in his military uniform, probably home on leave from the front, just long enough to make promises he hopes he can keep. Together, they are a fragile gift of beauty against the grit of war.

A waiter pauses at the table, his voice gentle, asking, "Another cup?"

The café is a sanctuary, and this table its quiet anchor. Fingers have traced its edges in longing; elbows have pressed against it in exhaustion. It holds the weight of stories in its grain marked by scars etched in love and loss…invisible yet indelible.

Outside, the world churns forward: fears, hopes, dreams, tears, laughter. In this city torn by war, even silence carries its own story…

And, as always, the table remembers.

The Seeds of Tomorrow

As I sit, reflecting on the extraordinary Ukrainian women whose lives fill these pages, I am struck by one undeniable truth: Ukraine's resilience is carved from their strength. These women—mothers, daughters, soldiers, healers, dreamers—people you've never heard of—are not merely enduring this war; they are shaping its legacy. Through their hands, their voices, their heartbreak, and their grit, they ensure that Ukraine remains unbroken.

In their quiet acts of defiance and monumental acts of courage, they teach us what it means to persevere. They remind us that humanity thrives not in the absence of hardship but in our response to it. As Viktor Frankl, a Holocaust survivor, observed: while we cannot always control what happens to us, we retain the freedom to choose how we respond. These women embody this truth, showing us that even in the darkest times, beauty and hope persist, woven into the fabric of loss and survival.

This book is a testament to them, not just as symbols of courage but as individuals with stories that deserve to be heard and honored. Their lives challenge us to confront our own definitions of strength and solidarity. They ask us to care, to act, to never forget.

To the women of Ukraine: you are the light in the shadows. Your stories will echo far beyond these pages, inspiring those who read them to believe in a future worth fighting for. And to the world: let us remember that in these women's courage lies the essence of freedom itself.

My hope is that you will carry their stories forward—not as distant observers but as active participants in building a world where no voice goes unheard and no sacrifice is in vain.

Christopher Briscoe

Books by Christopher Briscoe

Shifting Gears
Common Ground
Connections
The Road Between Us
Deux
The Spirit of New Orleans
The Stormy Legacy of Windansea
The Child on the Train
Dancing With the Waves
The Women of Ukraine

www.ShiftingGearsPub.com
www.ChrisBriscoe.com

Christopher Briscoe is a storyteller and a photographer, fueled by a profound belief that every person harbors a unique tale waiting to be unveiled. His compelling journey weaves a tapestry that spans the globe—from the solemn echoes of Death Row in Oregon to the vibrant streets of New Orleans, the bustling alleys of Bangkok, the diverse cultures of India and Ethiopia, to the front lines of battle-scarred Ukraine. Each photograph and story he shares uncovers the depth and resilience behind every face and landscape.

The author of several compelling books, his work stands as a bridge connecting diverse human experiences.

Residing in Ashland, Oregon, he continues to share stories that highlight our common humanity.

For further insight into Christopher Briscoe's work or to get in touch with him, visit www.shiftinggearspub.com.

The Women of Ukraine - Stories of Hope and Courage in a War-torn Country

Copyright © 2025 by Christopher Briscoe

All Rights Reserved. No part of this book may be reproduced in any written, electronic, recorded, or photocopied form without written permission of the publisher or author. The exception would be in the case of brief quotations embodied in critical articles or reviews and pages where permission is specifically granted by the publisher or author.

Interior & cover designs: Shifting Gears Publications.

ISBN: 979-8-9909755-3-8

Printed in the United States of America

Heartfelt Thanks

To Carole and David Florian, aka "The Team": Your friendship, sharp eyes, and endless encouragement keep me going. Your refusal to let me settle for anything less than my best has been both a blessing and a challenge. You deserve medals—truly.

To Davis Wilkins for the nudge to write this book.

To Lera: Thank you for being a friend, translator, videographer, and story hunter extraordinaire. You've uncovered tales that even Sherlock Holmes would envy, and you made the impossible feel possible.

To Roxalana, Bogdana, Natalia, and Lyuda: Your friendship, inspiration, and unwavering bravery remind me daily why these stories need to be told. You are the heart of this book.

www.ingramcontent.com/pod-product-compliance
Lightning Source LLC
Chambersburg PA
CBRC091935130526
44582CB00050B/188